ChatGPT Money Machine

Machine

Making AI Work for You

Kiet Huynh

Table of Contents

Introduction

Why ChatGPT?

In a world driven by constant technological advancements, artificial intelligence has emerged as a powerful tool that can transform the way we live and work. ChatGPT, an advanced language model developed by OpenAI, is at the forefront of this AI revolution. But why ChatGPT? What makes it so compelling and essential for today's users?

ChatGPT offers a multitude of benefits that make it a valuable asset for individuals, businesses, researchers, and many more. Here are some specific reasons why ChatGPT stands out:

1. Versatility: ChatGPT is not confined to a single use case. It's a versatile AI that can be adapted to serve a wide range of purposes. Whether you need assistance with research, content creation, problem-solving, or creative brainstorming, ChatGPT can adapt to your needs.

2. Efficiency: Time is a precious resource, and ChatGPT can help you save it. It quickly generates responses and assists you in various tasks, making you more productive.

3. Accessibility: ChatGPT is accessible to anyone with an internet connection. You don't need specialized knowledge or resources to harness its power.

4. Innovation: ChatGPT fosters innovation by sparking creativity and aiding in idea generation. It can be a valuable partner for writers, artists, and inventors.

5. Problem Solving: ChatGPT can help you solve complex problems, whether they're technical, educational, or related to healthcare. It provides insights and suggestions that can lead to solutions.

6. Ethical Use: Understanding the ethical implications of AI is crucial. ChatGPT is a tool for responsible AI use, and this book will guide you on ethical considerations and best practices.

This book, " ChatGPT Money Machine: Making AI Work for You," is designed to help you harness the potential of ChatGPT. In the following chapters, we will explore the various ways ChatGPT can be a valuable assistant in your personal and professional life, and provide you with practical insights and advice on using this technology to its fullest extent. Whether you're a seasoned AI user or just getting started, this book is your gateway to unlocking the power of ChatGPT. Let's embark on this journey together and discover how AI can truly work for you.

Getting Started with ChatGPT

Now that you understand why ChatGPT is a game-changer, it's time to dive into the world of this remarkable AI companion. This section will guide you through the process of getting started with ChatGPT.

1. Creating Your Account

- Before you can begin using ChatGPT, you'll need to create an account. We'll walk you through the registration process, including any necessary subscriptions and account settings.

2. Choosing the Right ChatGPT Plan

- ChatGPT offers various pricing plans, from free access to premium subscriptions. We'll help you choose the plan that aligns with your needs and budget.

3. Accessing ChatGPT

- Learn how to access ChatGPT through web interfaces, applications, or other platforms, depending on your chosen access method.

4. Setting Up Your Profile

- Personalize your ChatGPT experience by customizing your profile, including your preferred language, name, and any unique settings you desire.

5. Understanding Usage Limits

- ChatGPT usage often comes with certain limits, depending on your subscription. We'll explain these limits and how to manage your usage effectively.

6. Navigating the Chat Interface

- Familiarize yourself with the chat interface and how to communicate with ChatGPT effectively. We'll provide tips for maintaining a smooth and productive conversation.

7. Safety and Privacy

- Learn about the safety features and privacy options available when using ChatGPT, and how to ensure a secure experience.

8. Troubleshooting and Support

- Should you encounter issues, we'll guide you through common troubleshooting steps and how to seek support when needed.

By the end of this section, you'll be well-equipped to start your journey with ChatGPT. You'll understand why ChatGPT is worth your attention and how to make the most of it, regardless of your background or experience level. So, let's take the next step and explore the world of ChatGPT to see how it can truly work for you.

CHAPTER I
ChatGPT Basics

1.1 What is ChatGPT?

ChatGPT is a groundbreaking artificial intelligence language model developed by OpenAI. At its core, ChatGPT is an example of a generative language model, which means it's capable of understanding and generating human-like text based on the input it receives. What makes ChatGPT particularly remarkable is its size and scale, as it has been trained on vast amounts of text data from the internet, giving it a broad knowledge base.

Here are some key characteristics that define ChatGPT:

1. Generative Language Model: ChatGPT can generate coherent and contextually relevant text. You can provide it with prompts, questions, or text, and it will respond with meaningful content, which can be anything from answering questions to composing essays or even generating creative stories.

2. Large-Scale Training: ChatGPT's proficiency is the result of extensive training on diverse online text sources. This broad knowledge base allows it to handle a wide range of topics and domains.

3. Adaptability: ChatGPT can be adapted for various applications, from customer support chatbots to creative writing assistants, depending on how it's fine-tuned and customized.

4. Natural Language Processing: ChatGPT excels in understanding and generating human language. It can comprehend nuances, context, and even follow a conversation thread, making it suitable for natural and engaging interactions.

5. Wide Accessibility: ChatGPT is designed to be accessible to a wide audience. Users with varying degrees of technical expertise can make use of its capabilities through web interfaces, API integrations, and more.

6. Continual Improvement: OpenAI continuously refines and updates ChatGPT, making it more effective and safer. Feedback from users plays a significant role in this iterative process.

7. Potential and Limitations: While ChatGPT is powerful, it has limitations, including the potential to generate inappropriate or biased content. Understanding these limitations is essential for responsible use.

Understanding what ChatGPT is and what it can do is the first step in unlocking its potential. As we delve deeper into this chapter, we will explore how ChatGPT works, its interface, and how you can tailor your experience to best suit your needs, making it a valuable ally in various aspects of your life.

1.2 How ChatGPT Works

To comprehend how ChatGPT operates, it's essential to look under the hood and understand the underlying mechanisms that drive its functionality. At its core, ChatGPT relies on a few key concepts:

1. Deep Learning: ChatGPT employs a deep neural network architecture, specifically a variant of the Transformer model. This architecture enables it to process and generate text by learning patterns and relationships within large datasets.

2. Training Data: ChatGPT's proficiency is a result of its training on an extensive corpus of text data, including books, articles, websites, and more. During training, the model learns to predict the next word in a sentence, which helps it understand context and generate coherent responses.

3. Attention Mechanisms: The Transformer model employs attention mechanisms that allow it to focus on relevant parts of the input text. This attention to context is what enables ChatGPT to provide contextually appropriate responses in a conversation.

4. Fine-Tuning: While the base model is trained on a broad dataset, fine-tuning is a crucial step that tailors ChatGPT for specific tasks or applications. This process helps make the model more controlled and suited to your needs.

5. Generation and Sampling: ChatGPT generates text using a sampling technique. It can generate text word by word, making probabilistic choices for each word based on its understanding of the context. This randomness can sometimes result in variations in responses.

6. Prompt and Context: The input you provide, also known as a prompt or conversation context, plays a significant role in shaping ChatGPT's responses. Clear and well-structured prompts tend to yield more precise answers.

7. OpenAI's Continuous Updates: ChatGPT is not a static model. OpenAI regularly updates and fine-tunes it to improve performance, safety, and address issues.

Understanding these foundational aspects of ChatGPT's operation will help you communicate effectively with the model and get the most out of it. The subsequent sections of this chapter will delve into the practical aspects of using ChatGPT, including how to interact with its interface, customize your experience, and harness its power for your specific needs.

1.3 Understanding the ChatGPT Interface

The ChatGPT interface is your gateway to harnessing the power of AI for various purposes. In this section, we will delve into the details of how to effectively navigate and utilize the ChatGPT interface to achieve your specific goals. By the end of this section, you will have a clear understanding of the interface's key components and functionalities, along with practical examples of its use.

Key Components of the ChatGPT Interface:

1. Input Box: The input box is where you provide instructions or queries to ChatGPT. You can start a conversation by typing a message or question in this box. Make sure your instructions are clear and specific to get the best results.

2. Output Area: The output area displays ChatGPT's responses to your inputs. It provides you with text-based answers, suggestions, or information based on the context you establish.

3. User Settings: Accessible through the settings icon, you can customize your ChatGPT experience. You can set parameters like response length, tone, and even prompt-specific instructions. Tailoring these settings can significantly impact the quality of the responses you receive.

4. Chat History: The chat history allows you to revisit and review the entire conversation with ChatGPT. It's a valuable resource for tracking the progression of your interaction and recalling earlier information.

Navigating the ChatGPT Interface:

To effectively use the ChatGPT interface, follow these steps:

Step 1: Setting the Context

- Start the conversation by providing a clear context. For example, if you're writing a story and need creative ideas, begin with a prompt like, "I need ideas for a fantasy novel involving dragons and wizards."

Step 2: Asking Clear Questions

- Ask questions or provide instructions in a concise and straightforward manner. If you seek information, phrase your queries clearly, such as "What is the capital of France?" or "Tell me about climate change."

Step 3: Experiment and Iterate

- Feel free to experiment and iterate. If ChatGPT's response isn't exactly what you need, you can modify your instructions and ask follow-up questions to refine the output.

Illustrative Examples:

1. *Content Generation:*

   - User: "I need an engaging introduction for an article on space exploration."

   - ChatGPT: "In the vast expanse of the cosmos, humans have embarked on a journey to uncover the mysteries of the universe..."

2. *Research Assistance:*

   - User: "Can you provide a summary of the key findings in the latest IPCC report?"

   - ChatGPT: "The latest IPCC report, published in 2022, highlights the urgency of addressing climate change and outlines key findings, including..."

Achievable Results:

- Increased efficiency in content creation.

- Quick access to information and data.

- Assistance in generating creative content.

- Clarity in communication for specific tasks.

Understanding the ChatGPT interface empowers you to maximize the potential of AI assistance, whether for writing, research, or various other applications. As you progress, you'll discover even more ways to leverage this versatile tool effectively.

1.4 Customizing Your ChatGPT Experience

Customization is the key to unlocking the full potential of ChatGPT. In this section, we will explore the various ways in which you can tailor your ChatGPT experience to meet your unique needs and preferences. From setting tone and language to influencing response length, we'll provide detailed instructions and real-world examples to help you achieve the desired outcomes.

1. Setting the Tone:

ChatGPT can adapt to different tones and styles of communication, making it suitable for various applications. Here's how you can customize the tone:

a. Formal Tone:

- To receive formal responses, specify your desired tone by using phrases like, "Please provide a formal response," or "I need this to sound professional."

b. Casual Tone:

- For a more relaxed tone, use instructions such as, "I want this to be friendly and informal," or "Can you respond in a conversational style?"

2. Influencing Response Length:

You have control over how concise or detailed ChatGPT's responses are. Adjust the response length according to your requirements:

a. Short and Concise:

- If you prefer short and to-the-point responses, you can set a character or word limit. For instance, "Limit your response to 100 words."

b. In-Depth Explanation:

- To get detailed and informative answers, you can instruct, "Please provide an in-depth explanation."

3. Specifying Language and Style:

You can customize the language and style in which ChatGPT responds, ensuring it aligns with your content needs:

a. Language Selection:

- If you require responses in a specific language, simply state, "Respond in French" or "Answer in Spanish."

b. Style Preferences:

- For content that needs to match a particular style guide or writing style, you can specify instructions like, "Write in APA style" or "Use a journalistic tone."

4. Contextual Prompts:

Providing context in your prompts can significantly enhance the quality and relevance of ChatGPT's responses. When customizing your experience, remember to give context when necessary. For instance:

a. Creative Writing:

  - User: "I'm writing a science fiction story about time travel. Please provide a conversation between two characters in the year 3025."

- ChatGPT: "Character 1: 'Time travel has revolutionized our world. Character 2: 'Absolutely, it's fascinating how history can be rewritten.'"

Achievable Results:

- Tailoring responses to match the desired tone and style.

- Getting responses that fit specific character or word limits.

- Receiving content in the language of your choice.

- Aligning responses with specific writing or formatting guidelines.

- Enhancing context-aware communication for creative writing, research, and more.

By customizing your ChatGPT experience, you can make AI work for you in a way that perfectly suits your needs. These customization options empower you to utilize ChatGPT effectively across a wide range of applications, from creative writing to research and beyond.

CHAPTER II
Communication with ChatGPT

2.1 Effective Ways to Communicate

Effective communication with ChatGPT is crucial to get the most out of your AI interactions. In this section, we'll explore specific strategies and techniques to guide you on how to communicate effectively with ChatGPT, ensuring you receive the responses you desire. We'll provide practical examples and illustrate the outcomes you can expect from using these strategies.

1. Starting with a Clear and Specific Prompt:

To elicit the most relevant responses, initiate your interaction with a clear and specific prompt. Instead of asking a broad question like, "Tell me about space," consider making it more precise, such as, "Can you explain the concept of black holes in astrophysics?"

Example:

- User: "Can you explain the concept of black holes in astrophysics?"

- ChatGPT Response: "Black holes are regions of spacetime exhibiting gravitational pull so strong that nothing, not even light, can escape their grasp..."

Outcome: You receive a detailed and informative explanation of black holes in astrophysics.

2. Using Complete Sentences:

While ChatGPT can understand fragmented sentences, using complete sentences often results in more coherent and informative responses. Rather than saying, "Benefits of solar energy," phrase it as a complete question, such as, "What are the benefits of using solar energy?"

Example:

- User: "What are the benefits of using solar energy?"

- ChatGPT Response: "Using solar energy offers numerous advantages, including reduced greenhouse gas emissions, lower electricity bills, and increased energy independence..."

Outcome: ChatGPT provides a well-structured and informative response.

3. Asking Follow-Up Questions:

Engage in a dynamic conversation with ChatGPT by asking follow-up questions. This helps clarify information and allows you to delve deeper into a topic.

Example:

- User: "What is climate change?"

- ChatGPT Response: "Climate change refers to long-term shifts in weather patterns."

- User: "What are the main causes of climate change?"

Outcome: You receive a comprehensive explanation of the causes of climate change.

4. Providing Context and Background:

When seeking assistance for a specific project or topic, offer ChatGPT context and background information. For instance, you can say, "I'm writing a blog about sustainable agriculture. Can you provide me with statistics on global food waste?"

Example:

- User: "I'm writing a blog about sustainable agriculture. Can you provide me with statistics on global food waste?"

- ChatGPT Response: "Certainly, here are the latest statistics on global food waste, including regional disparities and potential solutions..."

Outcome: ChatGPT generates relevant statistics tailored to your project.

5. Experiment and Iterate:

Don't hesitate to experiment and iterate your prompts if the initial response doesn't fully meet your needs. Refining your instructions can help you obtain the desired information or assistance.

Example:

- User: "What is the impact of deforestation on biodiversity?"

- ChatGPT Response: "Deforestation has a severe impact on biodiversity by destroying natural habitats."

- User: "Can you provide specific examples of endangered species affected by deforestation?"

Outcome: Through trial and error, you can achieve more accurate and helpful responses from ChatGPT.

6. Specify Desired Style or Format:

If your project requires a particular writing style or format, inform ChatGPT. For example, you can say, "Write a persuasive essay on renewable energy in MLA format."

Example:

- User: "Write a persuasive essay on renewable energy in MLA format."

- ChatGPT Response: ChatGPT generates content that aligns with the specified style and format guidelines.

Outcome: ChatGPT produces content in the requested style and format.

7. Being Polite and Respectful:

Maintaining a respectful tone and politeness in your interactions with ChatGPT fosters a positive and productive engagement.

Example:

- User: "Could you please provide an overview of the Industrial Revolution?"

- ChatGPT Response: "Certainly, here's an overview of the Industrial Revolution..."

Outcome: ChatGPT continues to provide assistance in a helpful and respectful manner.

By applying these effective communication strategies and techniques, you can ensure that your interactions with ChatGPT result in clear, tailored, and relevant responses, making the AI a valuable asset for various tasks and projects.

2.2 Asking Questions

Asking questions effectively is a fundamental skill when interacting with ChatGPT. This section will guide you through the art of formulating questions that yield precise and informative responses from the AI. You will learn how to structure your questions, provide context, and refine your queries to obtain the desired information or assistance.

1. Structuring Questions:

To elicit informative responses, it's essential to structure your questions clearly and concisely. Consider the following guidelines:

- Start with a relevant keyword: Begin your question with a keyword that relates to the topic you're interested in. For instance, if you're researching climate change, you can start with "climate change" in your question.

Example:

- User: "Climate change impacts on marine ecosystems?"

- ChatGPT Response: "Climate change has substantial impacts on marine ecosystems, including ocean acidification and shifts in sea temperatures."

Outcome: ChatGPT provides a detailed response focusing on the effects of climate change on marine ecosystems.

2. Use open-ended questions: Open-ended questions encourage ChatGPT to provide more comprehensive answers. Avoid yes/no questions and opt for questions that begin with "What," "Why," "How," or "Explain."

Example:

- User: "Why is renewable energy important for environmental sustainability?"

- ChatGPT Response: "Renewable energy is crucial for environmental sustainability because it reduces greenhouse gas emissions, decreases reliance on fossil fuels, and promotes cleaner energy sources."

Outcome: ChatGPT delivers a detailed explanation of the importance of renewable energy for environmental sustainability.

3. Clarify and specify: If your question relates to a specific aspect of a topic, clarify and specify the details you need.

Example:

- User: "Can you explain the economic impact of artificial intelligence on job markets in the United States?"

- ChatGPT Response: ChatGPT provides detailed information regarding the economic impact of AI on job markets in the United States.

Outcome: ChatGPT offers insights into the economic implications of AI on the U.S. job market.

4. Sequential questions: Sometimes, it's more effective to break down complex topics into sequential questions. Start with a general inquiry and then ask follow-up questions for a deeper dive.

Example:

- User: "Tell me about climate change."

- ChatGPT Response: "Climate change refers to long-term shifts in weather patterns."

- User: "What are the main causes of climate change?"

Outcome: You receive a comprehensive explanation of climate change and later get detailed insights into its causes.

5. Providing context: If your question requires context, provide it in a concise manner. Context helps ChatGPT understand your request better.

Example:

- User: "In the context of the Industrial Revolution, what were the key technological advancements in manufacturing?"

- ChatGPT Response: ChatGPT provides information on key technological advancements during the Industrial Revolution in the context of manufacturing.

Outcome: You receive information specifically related to the technological advancements in manufacturing during the Industrial Revolution.

By mastering the art of asking questions effectively, you can obtain precise and informative responses from ChatGPT, making it a powerful tool for research, information gathering, and problem-solving.

Providing context when interacting with ChatGPT is a powerful technique to receive more relevant and accurate responses. This section will guide you on how to effectively supply context, giving the AI a better understanding of your queries. You'll learn how to frame your questions within a specific context and the benefits of doing so.

1. Framing Questions within Context:

Providing context helps ChatGPT understand the purpose of your inquiry. When framing your questions, consider the following:

- Setting a scenario: Describe the situation or scenario your question pertains to. This could include the topic, background information, or a specific context.

Example:

- User: "In the context of a technology article about artificial intelligence, please explain the concept of machine learning."

- ChatGPT Response: ChatGPT provides a detailed explanation of machine learning within the context of a technology article about artificial intelligence.

Outcome: The response is tailored to the context you've provided, ensuring it's relevant to your article.

2. Providing Background Information:

When your question requires knowledge of a specific background or event, offer a brief summary or relevant details to guide ChatGPT in its response.

Example:

- User: "In the context of the Vietnam War, can you explain the key events that led to the conflict?"

- ChatGPT Response: ChatGPT offers an explanation of the key events that led to the Vietnam War within the context of that historical conflict.

Outcome: You receive an accurate and comprehensive account of the events leading to the Vietnam War.

3. Explaining Your Goal:

Clearly communicate the goal or objective of your question. This helps ChatGPT understand the specific information or assistance you're seeking.

Example:

- User: "I'm working on a research project about renewable energy. In this context, please provide information on the latest advancements in solar panel technology."

- ChatGPT Response: ChatGPT provides information on the latest advancements in solar panel technology, aligning with the context of your research project on renewable energy.

Outcome: The response is well-aligned with the research project's goals, offering pertinent information.

4. Incorporating Specific Parameters:

Include specific parameters or constraints if your question depends on certain conditions. This narrows down the scope and improves response accuracy.

Example:

- User: "Within the context of a 1000-word blog post, explain the impact of deforestation on biodiversity."

- ChatGPT Response: ChatGPT generates an explanation of the impact of deforestation on biodiversity while adhering to the 1000-word limit for a blog post.

Outcome: The response is tailored to your specified context and word limit.

5. Benefit of Context:

Providing context enhances the relevance of responses from ChatGPT. It ensures that the AI understands the specific framework within which you need information or assistance, resulting in more accurate and valuable answers.

By incorporating these techniques for providing context in your questions, you can effectively guide ChatGPT to deliver responses that align with your goals and requirements. This makes the AI a valuable tool for tasks such as research, content creation, and problem-solving.

2.4 Maintaining a Natural Conversation Flow

Maintaining a natural conversation flow is a crucial aspect of effective interaction with ChatGPT. This section will provide you with strategies and techniques to ensure your conversations with the AI remain coherent and flowing smoothly. You'll learn how to engage in dynamic dialogues and keep the conversation on track.

1. Using Contextual References:

Refer back to previous parts of the conversation to keep the context clear and maintain a natural flow. Use pronouns like "it," "they," or "this" to refer to previous topics or messages.

Example:

- User: "What are the different types of renewable energy sources?"

- ChatGPT Response: "Renewable energy sources include solar, wind, hydro, and geothermal. Solar panels are a popular choice for residential applications because they are cost-effective."

- User: "Tell me more about their cost-effectiveness."

Outcome: The reference to "their cost-effectiveness" keeps the conversation on the same topic, allowing for a seamless transition to a related detail.

2. Structuring Follow-Up Questions:

When asking follow-up questions, structure them logically based on the AI's previous response. This ensures the conversation flows smoothly from one point to the next.

Example:

- User: "Can you explain the concept of machine learning?"

- ChatGPT Response: "Machine learning is a subset of artificial intelligence that focuses on training computer systems to learn from data."

- User: "How does the training process work?"

Outcome: The follow-up question smoothly continues the discussion by seeking further clarification on the training process.

3. Acknowledging Responses:

Acknowledge and respond to ChatGPT's answers to maintain a natural conversation. Express appreciation or seek additional details to show your engagement.

Example:

- User: "What is the capital of France?"

- ChatGPT Response: "The capital of France is Paris."

- User: "Thank you! Can you also tell me about its famous landmarks?"

Outcome: The expression of gratitude and the follow-up question help sustain the conversational flow.

4. Using Transition Phrases:

Incorporate transition phrases like "Furthermore," "Moreover," or "Additionally" to smoothly link related ideas and maintain a natural progression in the conversation.

Example:

- User: "What are the environmental benefits of recycling?"

- ChatGPT Response: "Recycling reduces landfill waste and conserves resources. Furthermore, it lowers greenhouse gas emissions."

Outcome: The use of "Furthermore" connects related environmental benefits of recycling.

5. Navigating Multiple Topics:

If the conversation covers multiple topics, clearly delineate when you are transitioning to a new subject. This helps prevent confusion and keeps the conversation organized.

Example:

- User: "Tell me about space exploration."

- ChatGPT Response: "Space exploration involves the use of spacecraft to study celestial objects. On a related note, the first moon landing was a monumental achievement."

Outcome: The user's transition to a related topic maintains clarity and coherence.

By implementing these strategies, you can ensure that your conversations with ChatGPT flow naturally, making interactions more engaging and productive. Maintaining a coherent dialogue enables you to explore various topics and gather information seamlessly.

CHAPTER III
Productivity and Efficiency

3.1 Using ChatGPT for Research

Leveraging ChatGPT for research purposes can significantly enhance your productivity and the depth of your investigations. In this section, we will delve into how to harness the power of ChatGPT for research projects. You will learn specific techniques, approaches, and best practices to extract valuable insights and information from the AI.

1. Defining Your Research Goals:

To get the most out of ChatGPT, it's essential to have clear research objectives. Begin by defining your research questions or the specific information you seek.

Example:

- User: "I'm researching the impact of climate change on coral reefs. Can you provide an overview of the current challenges faced by coral reefs due to climate change?"

Outcome: By specifying your research topic and questions, you set the stage for ChatGPT to provide relevant information.

2. Narrowing Down Your Focus:

In research, specificity is key. When interacting with ChatGPT, be sure to focus on particular aspects of your topic to obtain in-depth insights.

Example:

- User: "I'm studying renewable energy technologies. Can you explain the advancements in photovoltaic solar cells over the past decade?"

Outcome: By narrowing your focus to photovoltaic solar cells, ChatGPT can provide detailed information about advancements in this specific technology.

3. Citing Sources and References:

When engaging ChatGPT for research, ask the AI to provide citations or references for the information it generates. This ensures the credibility and reliability of the data.

Example:

- User: "Can you provide sources or references for the statistics on global carbon emissions in 2022?"

Outcome: Requesting sources helps verify the accuracy of the data and supports your research.

4. Collaborative Research:

ChatGPT can assist with collaborative research by generating ideas, summaries, or drafts that can be used by research teams. Share your research goals and collaborate effectively with the AI.

Example:

- User: "I'm part of a research team investigating the potential of sustainable agriculture. Can you provide an overview of sustainable farming practices and their environmental benefits?"

Outcome: ChatGPT contributes to collaborative research efforts by supplying valuable insights and content.

5. Review and Refinement:

After receiving information from ChatGPT, review and refine the content as needed to align with your research objectives. You can edit and expand upon the AI-generated content.

Example:

- User: "I'm researching the history of the Industrial Revolution. Can you provide a summary of the key inventions during that era?"

Outcome: ChatGPT generates an initial summary, which you can review, edit, and expand upon to create a comprehensive research document.

6. Data Collection and Analysis:

ChatGPT can assist in data collection by generating surveys, questionnaires, or interview questions, and it can help in analyzing data by summarizing findings or identifying patterns.

Example:

- User: "I'm conducting a market research survey. Can you help me create a set of questions to gather consumer preferences for electric vehicles?"

Outcome: ChatGPT generates a list of questions that you can use to collect valuable data from your target audience.

7. Literature Review and Summaries:

When conducting literature reviews, you can request ChatGPT to summarize research papers, articles, or books on your topic of interest.

Example:

- User: "I'm reviewing academic papers on quantum physics. Can you provide summaries of the key findings in these three research articles?"

Outcome: ChatGPT generates concise summaries of the research articles, saving you time in your literature review.

8. Generating Bibliographies and References:

ChatGPT can assist in formatting and generating bibliographies or lists of references in various citation styles.

Example:

- User: "I need to create a Chicago style bibliography for my research paper on urban planning. Can you help me format the citations correctly?"

Outcome: ChatGPT generates a correctly formatted Chicago style bibliography for your research paper.

9. Ethical Considerations:

When using ChatGPT for research, be mindful of ethical considerations, including proper citation and the responsible use of AI-generated content.

Example:

- User: "I want to ensure that I'm ethically using AI for my research. Can you provide guidelines on citing AI-generated content in academic papers?"

Outcome: ChatGPT offers guidance on ethical AI usage, including proper citation practices.

10. Continuous Iteration:

Remember that research is an iterative process. You can engage ChatGPT at various stages of your research to refine your approach and gather additional insights.

Example:

- User: "I've completed my initial research, but I need further insights into recent developments. Can you provide updates on advancements in renewable energy technologies?"

Outcome: ChatGPT supplies you with the latest information, helping you keep your research up to date.

11. Organizing and Synthesizing Information:

ChatGPT can assist you in organizing and synthesizing the data you collect during your research. You can request it to create structured summaries or reports that condense large amounts of information into a coherent format.

Example:

- User: "I've gathered a lot of data on market trends. Can you help me create a concise report summarizing the key findings?"

Outcome: ChatGPT generates a well-structured report that condenses the key findings from your research data.

12. Staying Informed:

To stay current in your field, you can use ChatGPT to provide you with regular updates on relevant topics, breaking news, or emerging research.

Example:

- User: "I want to stay updated on the latest developments in artificial intelligence. Can you send me weekly summaries of AI-related news and breakthroughs?"

Outcome: ChatGPT compiles and summarizes recent AI developments, keeping you informed and helping you stay ahead in your research.

13. Overcoming Research Challenges:

When facing roadblocks or challenges in your research, you can seek advice and insights from ChatGPT to overcome obstacles and generate new ideas.

Example:

- User: "I'm encountering difficulties in designing my research methodology. Can you provide guidance on effective research design for my study on urban planning?"

Outcome: ChatGPT offers guidance and suggests effective research design strategies to address your challenges.

14. Collaborative Research Assistance:

ChatGPT can facilitate collaborative research by generating collaborative documents, assisting with idea generation, and streamlining communication among team members.

Example:

- User: "I'm working on a collaborative research project with colleagues from different locations. Can you help us draft a project proposal and maintain a shared document for our research findings?"

Outcome: ChatGPT assists in the collaborative research process by generating a project proposal and maintaining a shared document for research findings.

15. Ethical and Responsible Research:

Remember to uphold ethical standards in your research, which includes appropriate data handling, responsible use of AI-generated content, and adherence to relevant research ethics guidelines.

Example:

- User: "I want to ensure our research project maintains high ethical standards. Can you provide guidelines on data privacy and responsible AI usage for our research team?"

Outcome: ChatGPT offers guidance on maintaining ethical standards in research, including data privacy and responsible AI usage.

By implementing these strategies, you can harness ChatGPT's capabilities to enhance your research efficiency, tackle challenges, and stay up to date in your field. The AI's capacity to provide accurate information and valuable insights makes it an indispensable tool for various research endeavors.

3.2 Content Generation and Writing Assistance

WelcomeChapter 3: Productivity and Efficiency

3.2 Content Generation and Writing Assistance

Leveraging ChatGPT for content generation and writing assistance can be a game-changer for authors, bloggers, and professionals looking to create high-quality content efficiently. In this section, we'll explore how to make the most of ChatGPT when it comes to content creation and writing support. You will learn specific strategies and best practices for generating compelling content with the help of the AI.

1. Generating Blog Posts and Articles:

ChatGPT can assist in creating blog posts and articles on a wide range of topics. You can provide guidance on the subject matter, style, and tone.

Example:

- User: "I need a blog post about the benefits of mindfulness meditation. Please write a 700-word article that explains its advantages for mental health."

Outcome: ChatGPT generates a well-structured article highlighting the benefits of mindfulness meditation, meeting the user's specified word count.

2. Crafting Compelling Product Descriptions:

When selling products or services, you can utilize ChatGPT to craft persuasive product descriptions that engage potential customers.

Example:

- User: "I'm launching a new line of organic skincare products. Can you create captivating product descriptions for our catalog?"

Outcome: ChatGPT generates product descriptions that highlight the unique features and benefits of the organic skincare products.

3. Creating Engaging Social Media Posts:

For social media marketing, ChatGPT can help generate attention-grabbing posts that resonate with your audience.

Example:

- User: "We're running a social media campaign for our fitness brand. Can you create engaging posts for our Instagram and Facebook profiles?"

Outcome: ChatGPT generates social media posts that are relevant to the fitness brand's campaign and aligned with the target platforms.

4. Assisting with Academic Writing:

Students and academics can benefit from ChatGPT's assistance in structuring essays, research papers, and academic articles.

Example:

- User: "I'm writing a research paper on climate change. Can you help me outline the introduction and key points for the paper?"

Outcome: ChatGPT provides an outline that includes the introduction and key points for the climate change research paper.

5. Writing Creative Fiction and Non-Fiction:

Writers and authors can use ChatGPT to brainstorm plot ideas, create character profiles, or develop dialogue for their creative works.

Example:

- User: "I'm working on a science fiction novel. Can you help me brainstorm ideas for the story's setting and technology?"

Outcome: ChatGPT offers creative suggestions for the novel's setting and technology, sparking the user's imagination.

6. Improving Writing Style and Clarity:

ChatGPT can assist in refining your writing style, making it more concise, clear, and engaging.

Example:

- User: "I've written a sales pitch, but it needs to be more persuasive. Can you help me revise it for maximum impact?"

Outcome: ChatGPT provides a revised sales pitch that enhances its persuasive power and clarity.

7. Multilingual Content Generation:

You can request ChatGPT to generate content in various languages to reach a global audience.

Example:

- User: "I want to create content about travel destinations in Spanish. Can you provide descriptions for popular destinations in Latin America?"

Outcome: ChatGPT generates content in Spanish, catering to the user's specific audience and language requirements.

8. Automated Newsletter Creation:

For businesses and organizations, ChatGPT can streamline the process of creating newsletters by generating content for updates, announcements, or informational newsletters.

Example:

- User: "We need a monthly newsletter for our subscribers. Can you draft content for our upcoming newsletter, including company updates and featured products?"

Outcome: ChatGPT generates content for the newsletter, simplifying the newsletter creation process.

9. Scriptwriting and Storytelling:

You can use ChatGPT to assist in scriptwriting for videos, podcasts, or storytelling for various media.

Example:

- User: "I'm producing a podcast episode. Can you help me create a script for the introduction and main talking points?"

Outcome: ChatGPT provides a script for the podcast episode introduction and main content, enhancing the user's podcast production.

10. Editing and Proofreading Assistance:

ChatGPT can assist with editing and proofreading content, helping you identify and correct grammatical errors and improve overall quality.

Example:

- User: "I've written a press release. Can you help me proofread and edit it for clarity and accuracy?"

Outcome: ChatGPT reviews and edits the press release, enhancing its readability and correctness.

11. Customizing Content for Your Brand:

You can guide ChatGPT in creating content that aligns with your brand's voice, values, and identity. This ensures consistency across your marketing materials.

Example:

- User: "We need content that resonates with our brand's eco-friendly image. Can you craft product descriptions that highlight sustainability and environmental consciousness?"

Outcome: ChatGPT generates product descriptions that emphasize eco-friendliness and align with the user's brand image.

12. Generating Email Campaign Content:

For email marketing campaigns, ChatGPT can assist in creating compelling email copy that encourages opens, click-throughs, and conversions.

Example:

- User: "We're launching a new product and need email content to promote it to our subscribers. Can you help us draft persuasive email copy?"

Outcome: ChatGPT generates email content that promotes the new product effectively and encourages subscriber engagement.

13. Tailoring Content for Specific Audiences:

ChatGPT can generate content that targets specific audience segments, such as creating content for different age groups, demographics, or interests.

Example:

- User: "We want to reach a younger audience with our social media content. Can you create posts that resonate with Gen Z and Millennials?"

Outcome: ChatGPT generates social media content that appeals to the specified younger audience segments.

14. Ideation and Brainstorming:

The AI can assist in brainstorming ideas for content topics, headlines, or creative concepts.

Example:

- User: "We're planning our content calendar for the next quarter. Can you provide ideas for blog post topics and catchy headlines?"

Outcome: ChatGPT generates a list of blog post topics and headlines that inspire creative content planning.

15. Managing Content Workflows:

For businesses and content teams, ChatGPT can streamline content creation workflows by generating drafts, outlines, or templates for various content types.

Example:

- User: "We're launching a content marketing campaign. Can you help us create a content calendar and outline for our blog posts, videos, and infographics?"

Outcome: ChatGPT generates a content calendar and outlines for various content types, simplifying the content creation process.

16. Ethical and Responsible Content Creation:

Remember to use AI-generated content ethically and responsibly. Ensure it complies with copyright, plagiarism, and content guidelines.

Example:

- User: "We want to maintain ethical content practices. Can you provide guidelines on using AI-generated content in a responsible and compliant manner?"

Outcome: ChatGPT offers guidelines on the responsible use of AI-generated content, supporting ethical content creation.

17. Enhancing SEO and Keywords:

ChatGPT can assist in optimizing content for search engines by generating keyword-rich content, meta descriptions, and title tags.

Example:

- User: "We need to improve our website's SEO. Can you create meta descriptions and title tags for our key product pages?"

Outcome: ChatGPT generates SEO-friendly meta descriptions and title tags, enhancing the website's search engine visibility.

18. Adapting to Content Trends:

Stay updated with the latest content trends and ask ChatGPT to generate content that aligns with current industry standards.

Example:

- User: "Our content needs to align with current design trends. Can you help us create blog posts with content that reflects the latest design aesthetics?"

Outcome: ChatGPT generates content that incorporates current design trends, keeping your content relevant.

19. Automating Social Media Scheduling:

Utilize ChatGPT to schedule social media content, helping you maintain a consistent online presence.

Example:

- User: "We want to automate our social media posts. Can you help us schedule a month's worth of posts for our business page?"

Outcome: ChatGPT schedules a month's worth of social media posts, saving time and ensuring consistent posting.

20. Generating Sales and Marketing Copy:

Craft persuasive sales and marketing copy for landing pages, product descriptions, and advertisements to drive conversions.

Example:

- User: "We need compelling ad copy for our upcoming product launch. Can you create ads that grab the audience's attention and drive sales?"

Outcome: ChatGPT generates attention-grabbing ad copy that enhances conversion rates.

21. Creating User Manuals and Documentation:

For businesses and software companies, ChatGPT can assist in generating user manuals, documentation, and instructional guides.

Example:

- User: "We're launching a new software product. Can you help us create a user manual to guide customers on its use?"

Outcome: ChatGPT generates a comprehensive user manual that assists customers in using the software effectively.

22. Assisting with Grant Proposals:

Nonprofits and researchers can utilize ChatGPT to assist in grant proposal writing, ensuring clarity and persuasiveness.

Example:

- User: "We're applying for a research grant. Can you help us draft a compelling proposal that highlights the significance of our project?"

Outcome: ChatGPT provides a persuasive grant proposal that enhances the project's chances of funding.

23. Crafting Email Newsletters:

Engage your audience with well-crafted email newsletters by utilizing ChatGPT to generate engaging content.

Example:

- User: "We need a monthly email newsletter for our subscribers. Can you help us create content that keeps them informed and engaged?"

Outcome: ChatGPT generates newsletter content that informs and engages subscribers.

24. Maintaining Consistency in Branding:

Ensure that the content generated aligns with your brand's voice, style, and messaging across various channels.

Example:

- User: "We want consistent branding across our content. Can you generate content that reflects our brand's personality and values?"

Outcome: ChatGPT produces content that maintains brand consistency, strengthening brand identity.

By incorporating these strategies, you can unlock the full potential of ChatGPT for content generation and writing assistance, streamlining your content creation process, and enhancing the effectiveness of your marketing and communication efforts. The AI's ability to generate persuasive and audience-focused content makes it a valuable asset for a wide range of content creators and businesses...

3.3 Data Analysis and Interpretation

WelcomeChapter 3: Productivity and Efficiency

3.3 Data Analysis and Interpretation

In this section, we will explore how ChatGPT can be a valuable tool for data analysis and interpretation, providing a detailed guide on how to leverage its capabilities effectively.

Understanding Data Analysis with ChatGPT:

- ChatGPT can assist users in analyzing and interpreting data, whether it's numerical data, textual information, or complex datasets. It can provide insights, generate reports, and help draw meaningful conclusions.

Example:

- User: "I have a dataset with customer survey responses. Can you help me analyze the data to identify trends and preferences?"

Outcome: ChatGPT analyzes the survey data, identifies key trends, and provides a report on customer preferences.

Data Visualization and Presentation:

- ChatGPT can assist in creating data visualizations and presentations, helping users convey data-driven insights effectively.

Example:

- User: "We need a compelling presentation of our quarterly sales data. Can you help create charts and slides to illustrate the trends?"

Outcome: ChatGPT generates charts and slides that visually represent the quarterly sales data, enhancing the presentation.

Statistical Analysis and Hypothesis Testing:

- Users can request ChatGPT to perform statistical analyses and hypothesis testing on datasets to validate or reject hypotheses.

Example:

- User: "We're conducting a research study, and we need to perform hypothesis testing. Can you help us determine the statistical significance of our findings?"

Outcome: ChatGPT conducts hypothesis testing, determining the statistical significance of research findings.

Natural Language Processing for Textual Data:

- ChatGPT can process and analyze textual data, providing sentiment analysis, topic modeling, and other NLP-related tasks.

Example:

- User: "We have a collection of customer reviews. Can you analyze the sentiment and identify common topics mentioned in the reviews?"

Outcome: ChatGPT performs sentiment analysis and identifies common topics in the customer reviews.

Machine Learning Model Interpretation:

- ChatGPT can help users interpret machine learning models, explaining the factors and features that influence model predictions.

Example:

- User: "We're using a machine learning model for predicting customer churn. Can you help us interpret the model's predictions and the key factors contributing to churn?"

Outcome: ChatGPT provides an interpretation of the machine learning model's predictions and highlights the key factors influencing customer churn.

Quality Control and Anomaly Detection:

- ChatGPT can assist in quality control by identifying anomalies and irregularities in datasets, ensuring data accuracy.

Example:

- User: "We have a dataset of product measurements. Can you help us identify and flag any anomalous measurements that may affect quality control?"

Outcome: ChatGPT identifies and flags anomalous measurements within the dataset, supporting quality control efforts.

Predictive Analytics and Forecasting:

- ChatGPT can assist in predictive analytics, generating forecasts and insights for future trends based on historical data.

Example:

- User: "We want to forecast sales for the next quarter. Can you generate predictions and insights based on our historical sales data?"

Outcome: ChatGPT provides sales forecasts and insights for the next quarter based on historical sales data.

Interpreting Complex Datasets:

- ChatGPT can help users interpret complex and multifaceted datasets, making sense of interconnected variables and relationships.

Example:

- User: "We have a dataset with multiple variables. Can you help us understand the relationships and dependencies between these variables?"

Outcome: ChatGPT provides insights into the relationships and dependencies within the complex dataset.

Ethical Data Analysis Practices:

- ChatGPT can guide users on ethical data analysis practices, ensuring data privacy, responsible use of AI-generated insights, and compliance with data protection regulations.

Example:

- User: "We want to maintain ethical data analysis practices. Can you provide guidelines on data privacy and the responsible use of AI-generated insights?"

Outcome: ChatGPT offers guidelines on ethical data analysis, including data privacy and responsible AI usage.

Optimizing Business Decisions:

- Users can rely on ChatGPT to assist in making informed business decisions based on data analysis. By providing data-driven insights, the AI can help in strategic planning, resource allocation, and risk assessment.

Example:

- User: "We're deciding on the expansion of our product line. Can you provide data-driven insights on market trends and customer preferences to support our decision-making?"

Outcome: ChatGPT offers insights on market trends, customer preferences, and other relevant data, aiding in the decision-making process.

Customized Data Reports:

- ChatGPT can generate customized data reports tailored to specific business needs. These reports may include key performance indicators, trend analyses, and recommendations.

Example:

- User: "We need a monthly performance report for our e-commerce platform. Can you generate a report that includes sales figures, conversion rates, and suggestions for improvement?"

Outcome: ChatGPT generates a comprehensive performance report with sales figures, conversion rates, and improvement suggestions.

Analyzing Market Competitors:

- Users can request ChatGPT to analyze competitors' data and extract insights to gain a competitive advantage.

Example:

- User: "We want to understand our competitors' pricing strategies. Can you analyze their pricing data and provide insights?"

Outcome: ChatGPT analyzes competitors' pricing data and provides insights into their strategies.

Collaborative Data Interpretation:

- ChatGPT can be a valuable addition to collaborative data analysis and interpretation sessions, helping teams work together to extract insights.

Example:

- User: "Our data analysis team is working on a complex dataset. Can ChatGPT assist in collaborative sessions by explaining data trends and variables?"

Outcome: ChatGPT assists the team by explaining data trends and variables, enhancing collaborative analysis.

Data-Driven Content Creation:

- Users can utilize data insights from ChatGPT to create data-driven content, such as reports, articles, or marketing materials.

Example:

- User: "We want to write a data-driven industry report. Can ChatGPT provide insights to include in the report?"

Outcome: ChatGPT offers data insights to incorporate into the data-driven industry report.

Predictive Maintenance and IoT:

- In industrial settings, ChatGPT can support predictive maintenance efforts by analyzing IoT sensor data and identifying equipment maintenance needs.

Example:

- User: "We're implementing predictive maintenance for our manufacturing equipment. Can ChatGPT analyze sensor data and predict maintenance requirements?"

Outcome: ChatGPT analyzes sensor data, predicting maintenance needs and reducing equipment downtime.

Compliance and Regulatory Insights:

- ChatGPT can help users stay compliant with industry regulations and provide insights into regulatory changes.

Example:

- User: "We need to ensure regulatory compliance in our financial reporting. Can ChatGPT provide insights into relevant regulations and changes?"

Outcome: ChatGPT offers insights into financial regulations and changes, aiding in compliance efforts.

By incorporating ChatGPT into data analysis and interpretation processes, users can enhance their ability to extract meaningful insights from data, make informed decisions, and present data effectively. The AI's adaptability in handling various data-related tasks makes it a valuable asset for businesses, researchers, and professionals involved in data analysis and decision-making.

3.4 Automating Routine Tasks

WelcomeCertainly, here is the section on "Automating Routine Tasks" for Chapter 3: Productivity and Efficiency:

Automating Routine Tasks

ChatGPT is not only a valuable tool for generating content and conducting research; it can also be a powerful assistant in automating routine tasks, saving you time and effort. Whether you're a busy professional, a student, or someone seeking to streamline your daily responsibilities, ChatGPT can offer innovative solutions for task automation.

1. Email Management: ChatGPT can help you manage your emails more efficiently. It can sort, categorize, and draft responses to emails, ensuring that your inbox is organized and your communication is prompt.

2. Data Entry and Analysis: Repetitive data entry and analysis tasks can be time-consuming. ChatGPT can automate these processes, reducing the risk of human errors and accelerating data-related work.

3. Scheduling and Calendar Management: Let ChatGPT take over the hassle of scheduling appointments and managing your calendar. It can handle meeting requests, send reminders, and make sure your schedule runs smoothly.

4. Content Publishing: For bloggers, content creators, and social media managers, ChatGPT can be used to schedule and publish content. It can generate engaging social media posts and articles, allowing you to maintain a consistent online presence.

5. Customer Support: ChatGPT can assist in providing basic customer support by answering frequently asked questions, resolving common issues, and directing customers to the right resources.

6. Text Summarization: When dealing with lengthy documents or articles, ChatGPT can quickly summarize them, saving you the time and effort required to read through extensive content.

7. File Management: Automate file organization, backup, and archiving tasks. ChatGPT can help ensure your digital files are well-organized and easily accessible.

8. Data Retrieval: ChatGPT can fetch specific data or information from databases, websites, or documents, making it a handy tool for researchers and analysts.

9. Language Translation: If you frequently work with content in different languages, ChatGPT can help automate translation tasks, making your work more accessible to a global audience.

10. Scripting and Coding: For developers and programmers, ChatGPT can assist in generating code snippets, debugging, and automating certain coding tasks.

When automating routine tasks with ChatGPT, it's essential to provide clear instructions and guidelines to ensure accuracy and effectiveness. By offloading repetitive work to ChatGPT, you free up your time to focus on more strategic and creative aspects of your work or personal life. It's a prime example of how AI can be a valuable ally in boosting productivity and efficiency.

CHAPTER IV
Creativity and Innovation

4.1 Brainstorming Ideas with ChatGPT

Creativity is the cornerstone of innovation, and ChatGPT can be your trusty partner in brainstorming and generating innovative ideas. Whether you're a writer, designer, entrepreneur, or anyone seeking fresh perspectives, ChatGPT can help you tap into your creative potential and explore new horizons. In this chapter, we will delve into the art of brainstorming with ChatGPT, offering you concrete strategies and examples to unlock the full potential of your creative thought process.

1. Defining Your Creative Challenge

To start, it's essential to define the creative challenge or problem you want to tackle. Be as specific as possible. Are you looking for ideas for a new product, a marketing campaign, a novel plot, or a design project? The more clearly you can articulate the challenge, the better ChatGPT can assist you.

2. The Ideation Process

Brainstorming is about generating a multitude of ideas, even the seemingly outlandish ones. ChatGPT excels at ideation, offering a wide range of prompts, suggestions, and concepts. Here's how you can use ChatGPT effectively in the ideation process:

  - Keyword Prompting: Provide a few keywords related to your challenge. For example, if you're brainstorming a new marketing campaign for a tech startup, you can input keywords like "technology," "innovation," and "customer engagement." ChatGPT will then generate ideas based on these keywords.

- Creative Constraints: Sometimes, constraints can foster creativity. Specify constraints or limitations for your project, and let ChatGPT suggest ideas within those boundaries. This can lead to unique and innovative solutions.

- Collaborative Ideation: Collaborate with ChatGPT by engaging in a back-and-forth conversation. Pose questions, seek clarifications, and let ChatGPT respond with insights and suggestions. This dynamic exchange can often lead to unexpected and creative ideas.

3. Idea Refinement

Once you have a list of ideas, it's time to refine and evaluate them. Not all ideas will be equally viable or innovative. ChatGPT can assist in this phase by:

- Providing Context: Ask ChatGPT to provide context or background information for your ideas. This can help you better understand the potential impact and feasibility of each concept.

- Feedback and Evaluation: Seek ChatGPT's input on the pros and cons of various ideas. ChatGPT can analyze and compare ideas based on specific criteria, helping you identify the most promising ones.

- Combining Ideas: ChatGPT can suggest ways to merge or combine multiple ideas to create a hybrid concept. This often leads to innovative solutions that draw from diverse sources of inspiration.

4. Implementation and Action

Once you've refined your ideas, it's time to put them into action. ChatGPT can help you outline a plan, develop a project timeline, or even assist with writing proposals or business plans to bring your innovative ideas to life.

Case Study: From Concept to Reality

To illustrate the power of brainstorming with ChatGPT, let's consider a case study:

Scenario: You're a marketing manager tasked with creating a unique campaign for a sustainable fashion brand.

1. Defining the Challenge: Your challenge is to generate a marketing campaign that highlights the brand's commitment to sustainability while attracting a broader audience.

2. Ideation with ChatGPT: You provide keywords like "sustainability," "eco-friendly," and "fashion." ChatGPT suggests ideas such as a "Green Wardrobe Challenge," where customers are encouraged to recycle old clothing in exchange for discounts, or an "Eco-Fashion Show" featuring sustainable fashion designers.

3. Idea Refinement: You ask ChatGPT for feedback on the feasibility of these ideas and gather insights on how to implement them. ChatGPT helps you evaluate the potential impact and resource requirements.

4. Implementation: With ChatGPT's assistance, you develop a detailed plan for the "Green Wardrobe Challenge" campaign, including marketing materials, a timeline, and a promotional strategy.

In this case, brainstorming with ChatGPT has not only generated innovative ideas but also guided you through the process of turning those ideas into actionable plans.

Remember, the key to successful brainstorming with ChatGPT is to maintain an open and inquisitive mind. ChatGPT is a versatile tool that can adapt to various creative challenges, making it an invaluable asset for those seeking fresh and innovative ideas in any field. By harnessing ChatGPT's creative potential, you can drive innovation and make your projects stand out in a competitive landscape.

4.2 Creative Writing and Storytelling

ChatGPT is a versatile tool that can significantly enhance your creative writing and storytelling endeavors. Whether you're an aspiring author, content creator, or just someone looking to improve your writing skills, ChatGPT can be a valuable partner in the creative process. In this section, we will explore how ChatGPT can help you generate engaging stories, develop compelling characters, and improve your overall writing style.

1. Generating Story Ideas

ChatGPT can serve as a boundless source of inspiration for your creative writing projects. Here's how you can use ChatGPT to generate story ideas:

 - Prompts and Scenarios: Ask ChatGPT for story prompts or scenarios. Provide some initial context or themes to narrow down the suggestions. For example, if you're writing a science fiction story, you can request prompts related to space exploration or futuristic technology.

 - Character Development: ChatGPT can help you create well-rounded characters. Describe the traits, backgrounds, and motivations you envision for your characters, and ChatGPT can suggest additional details, quirks, or backstories to make your characters more vivid.

2. Plot Development and Outline

Once you have a story idea, ChatGPT can assist in developing a plot and outlining your narrative. Here's how to make the most of ChatGPT:

 - Plot Points and Twists: Engage ChatGPT in a conversation about your story idea, and it can suggest plot points, twists, and conflicts to keep your readers engaged.

- Story Arcs: ChatGPT can help you structure your story with a well-defined beginning, middle, and end. It can offer guidance on creating effective story arcs for different genres, whether it's a mystery, romance, or fantasy.

3. Writing Assistance

ChatGPT can act as your writing companion, helping you overcome writer's block and refining your prose:

- Overcoming Writer's Block: If you're stuck on a particular scene or need help with a challenging passage, describe your predicament to ChatGPT, and it can offer suggestions or even write a draft to get you started.

- Improving Descriptions and Dialogue: ChatGPT can provide guidance on enhancing descriptions, character dialogues, and narrative flow. It can offer suggestions for evocative language and realistic conversations.

- Editing and Proofreading: ChatGPT can help with editing and proofreading your work. Share a passage or an entire chapter, and it can offer suggestions for grammar, punctuation, and style improvements.

4. Genre-specific Guidance

ChatGPT's versatility extends to various genres and writing styles:

- Fiction and Non-fiction: Whether you're working on a novel, short story, essay, or memoir, ChatGPT can tailor its suggestions to match the genre and style of your writing.

- Genre Exploration: If you're looking to explore a new genre, ChatGPT can provide insights, tips, and genre-specific conventions to help you get started.

Case Study: Crafting a Compelling Short Story

Let's explore how ChatGPT can assist in crafting a compelling short story:

Scenario: You're a writer aiming to create an engaging mystery short story.

1. Generating Story Ideas: You ask ChatGPT for mystery story prompts. ChatGPT suggests a prompt involving a missing heirloom and a series of cryptic letters.

2. Plot Development and Outline: In your conversation with ChatGPT, you discuss the plot's key elements and possible suspects. ChatGPT offers ideas for plot twists and reveals.

3. Writing Assistance: You share a paragraph from your story, and ChatGPT provides suggestions to improve the pacing and descriptive elements. It also helps you fine-tune the dialogue between the detective and the suspects.

4. Genre-specific Guidance: You inquire about tips for writing a mystery story, and ChatGPT offers insights on creating suspense and planting clues effectively.

In this case, ChatGPT has guided you from the inception of your story idea through plot development, writing assistance, and genre-specific advice, resulting in a compelling mystery short story.

Harnessing ChatGPT's capabilities in creative writing and storytelling can elevate your narrative skills and inspire imaginative, engaging content. Whether you're a seasoned author or a novice writer, ChatGPT is a powerful ally in the pursuit of crafting captivating stories that resonate with your readers.

4.3 Design and Art Assistance

ChatGPT can be a valuable tool for artists and designers, providing creative support and guidance in various aspects of the design and art process. Whether you're a graphic designer, illustrator, or someone looking to explore your artistic side, ChatGPT can help you ideate, create, and improve your visual projects. In this section, we'll explore how ChatGPT can assist with design and art, from generating ideas to enhancing your work.

1. Idea Generation and Concept Development

ChatGPT can serve as an endless source of inspiration for your design and art projects. Here's how to leverage ChatGPT for idea generation:

- Visual Prompts: Describe the theme or concept you have in mind, and ChatGPT can suggest visual prompts and ideas that align with your vision. For example, if you're designing a poster for a music festival, you can provide details about the event, and ChatGPT can offer visual elements and concepts.

- Mood and Style Suggestions: If you're uncertain about the mood or style you want to convey in your artwork, ChatGPT can provide guidance on color schemes, themes, and artistic approaches based on your project's goals.

2. Design and Composition

Once you have a concept in mind, ChatGPT can assist in designing and composing your artwork:

- Layout and Composition: Describe the composition you're envisioning for your design, and ChatGPT can offer suggestions on how to arrange visual elements, text, and graphics to create an aesthetically pleasing piece.

- Color Palette and Typography: ChatGPT can help you select an appropriate color palette and typography that align with your design concept. It can recommend colors that complement each other and fonts that suit the project's tone.

3. Artistic Techniques and Styles

If you're exploring different artistic techniques and styles, ChatGPT can provide insights and guidance:

- Artistic Techniques: Seek advice on specific artistic techniques or effects, such as watercolor painting, digital illustration, or pointillism. ChatGPT can explain how to achieve these effects or offer tips on improving your skills.

- Art History and References: ChatGPT can suggest art movements, artists, or specific pieces that may inspire your work. It can provide historical context and references to help you gain a deeper understanding of art and design.

4. Problem Solving and Feedback

When you encounter challenges or uncertainties in your creative process, ChatGPT can offer problem-solving and feedback:

- Overcoming Creative Blocks: Describe the artistic challenge you're facing, whether it's a composition issue or a color choice dilemma. ChatGPT can provide suggestions to help you move forward.

- Feedback and Critique: Share your work with ChatGPT and ask for constructive feedback. ChatGPT can point out areas that may need improvement, offering suggestions for enhancing your art.

Case Study: Designing a Logo for a Sustainable Brand

Let's explore how ChatGPT can assist in designing a logo for a sustainable brand:

Scenario: You're a graphic designer tasked with creating a logo for an eco-friendly product line.

1. Idea Generation: You describe the brand's values and mission to ChatGPT. ChatGPT suggests ideas like using natural elements (leaves, water, or eco symbols) and provides visual references.

2. Design and Composition: You ask ChatGPT for tips on how to arrange these elements in a balanced and visually appealing way. ChatGPT offers suggestions on layout and color palette.

3. Artistic Techniques: You inquire about creating a watercolor effect for the logo. ChatGPT explains the technique and suggests digital tools for achieving the desired effect.

4. Problem Solving: You face a creative block in finalizing the design. ChatGPT offers advice on simplifying the logo and provides feedback to make it more impactful.

In this case, ChatGPT has guided you through the entire design process, from idea generation to finalizing the logo for a sustainable brand.

By collaborating with ChatGPT in your design and art projects, you can tap into its vast knowledge and creative potential to bring your artistic vision to life. Whether you're a professional designer or an amateur artist, ChatGPT can be an invaluable assistant in creating visually striking and meaningful art and designs.

4.4 Unlocking Creativity with ChatGPT

Creativity is a limitless wellspring of ideas, innovation, and imagination, and ChatGPT is the key to unlock this potential. Whether you're an artist, writer, entrepreneur, or simply someone seeking to tap into your creative side, ChatGPT can be your ultimate muse. In this section, we'll explore the various ways in which ChatGPT can unleash your creativity, helping you overcome mental blocks and sparking innovative ideas.

1. Exploring Uncharted Territories

ChatGPT can guide you into unexplored realms of creativity. Here's how to navigate these territories:

- Ideation Beyond Boundaries: ChatGPT can assist you in transcending the familiar by encouraging "out of the box" thinking. By providing abstract prompts and scenarios, ChatGPT can push your creative boundaries.

- Cross-disciplinary Inspiration: ChatGPT can introduce you to ideas and concepts from different fields. For instance, if you're a writer, ChatGPT can infuse scientific concepts into your storytelling, creating unique narratives.

2. Creative Challenges and Exercises

Engaging in creative challenges and exercises can stimulate your imagination and push your creative limits. ChatGPT can facilitate this process:

- Random Prompts and Constraints: Challenge ChatGPT to provide you with random prompts, constraints, or limitations. For instance, ask for a prompt for a short story that includes the words "whisper," "emerald," and "abandoned warehouse."

- Writing Sprints and Timed Exercises: Set a timer and engage in writing or art sprints with ChatGPT. The pressure of time can lead to spontaneous and creative breakthroughs.

3. Collaborative Creativity

Creativity often thrives in collaboration. ChatGPT can be your collaborative partner:

- Co-creative Storytelling: Collaborate with ChatGPT in real-time to co-write a story or brainstorm ideas. Engage in a dynamic back-and-forth exchange to fuel the creative process.

- Artistic Co-creation: Work with ChatGPT to generate visual art together. Describe your vision, and ChatGPT can help bring it to life, offering visual ideas and suggestions.

4. Learning and Improving Creative Skills

ChatGPT can be a tutor and mentor, helping you enhance your creative skills:

- Creative Writing Techniques: If you're a writer, ChatGPT can offer insights into various writing techniques, such as metaphor, symbolism, or character development, to elevate your storytelling.

- Artistic Advice: For artists, ChatGPT can provide guidance on improving your technical skills, exploring new styles, or mastering specific artistic techniques.

5. Overcoming Creative Blocks

Creative blocks are common hurdles in the creative process. ChatGPT can assist in overcoming these obstacles:

- Problem Solving: When you're stuck on a particular creative challenge, describe the problem to ChatGPT, and it can offer suggestions and solutions to help you move forward.

- Mindful Creativity: ChatGPT can guide you through mindfulness exercises and practices that promote relaxation and clarity, enabling you to access your creative wellspring.

Case Study: Exploring Multidisciplinary Creativity

Let's delve into a case study of how ChatGPT can help unlock multidisciplinary creativity:

Scenario: You're an artist and writer who wants to combine visual art and storytelling in a unique project.

1. Ideation Beyond Boundaries: You ask ChatGPT for a concept that fuses art and storytelling. ChatGPT suggests a multimedia project where you create visual art pieces and write accompanying short stories, each inspired by a famous painting.

2. Creative Challenges: You engage in a timed exercise, challenging yourself to create a piece of art and a short story in one hour. ChatGPT provides the prompt for this creative sprint, which involves a mysterious door and a lost key.

3. Collaborative Creativity: You and ChatGPT co-create a piece of artwork, with you describing the initial concept and ChatGPT offering visual ideas. Then, you write a story based on the created artwork, merging the two creative forms.

4. Learning and Improving Skills: As you work on your project, you seek advice from ChatGPT on improving your narrative and artistic skills. ChatGPT offers insights on character development and art techniques to enhance your project's quality.

In this case, ChatGPT has been instrumental in facilitating a multidisciplinary creative project, blending visual art and storytelling to explore uncharted creative territories.

With ChatGPT as your creative collaborator and mentor, you can transcend the limits of your imagination, turning your creative visions into reality. Whether you're an experienced artist or a novice in the world of creativity, ChatGPT is your companion in the journey to unlocking boundless creativity and innovative ideas.

CHAPTER V
Problem Solving

5.1 Troubleshooting and Technical Support

ChatGPT isn't just a source of creative inspiration; it's also a valuable ally when it comes to troubleshooting technical issues and providing support. Whether you're an individual encountering computer problems or an organization seeking assistance with software, ChatGPT can guide you through the process of diagnosing and resolving technical challenges efficiently and effectively. In this section, we'll explore how ChatGPT can be your go-to resource for troubleshooting and technical support.

1. Diagnosing Technical Issues

One of the first steps in resolving any technical problem is identifying the root cause. ChatGPT can assist in this diagnostic process:

- Problem Description: Describe the issue you're facing in as much detail as possible. Whether it's a software glitch, hardware malfunction, or network problem, articulate the symptoms and the context in which the issue occurred.

- Troubleshooting Steps: ChatGPT can suggest a series of troubleshooting steps based on the problem description you provide. These steps may include checking connections, verifying settings, and testing components.

2. Software and Hardware Support

ChatGPT can offer guidance on a wide range of software and hardware issues, such as:

- Operating System Problems: If you're encountering difficulties with your operating system (e.g., Windows, macOS, Linux), ChatGPT can provide instructions on resolving common issues like driver problems, updates, and system crashes.

- Software Glitches: When specific applications or software are not functioning correctly, ChatGPT can help you identify the cause and provide solutions. Whether it's troubleshooting a malfunctioning spreadsheet or a malfunctioning design software, ChatGPT can guide you through the process.

- Hardware Malfunctions: If you're experiencing hardware problems, ChatGPT can suggest diagnostics and steps to check for issues with components like your computer's hard drive, graphics card, or peripherals.

- Network Connectivity: For network-related problems, whether they're in a home or office setting, ChatGPT can assist in diagnosing issues with internet connectivity, router problems, or firewall settings.

3. Software and Tools Recommendations

ChatGPT can recommend software solutions and tools that may help resolve specific issues:

- Anti-virus and Security Tools: If you're concerned about cybersecurity, ChatGPT can suggest reliable anti-virus and security software to protect your devices.

- Data Recovery: If you've experienced data loss, ChatGPT can recommend data recovery software and provide guidance on how to use it.

- Productivity Software: ChatGPT can suggest productivity and organization tools to enhance your workflow and address software-related issues.

4. System Optimization

In addition to troubleshooting problems, ChatGPT can offer advice on optimizing your system for better performance:

- Cleanup and Maintenance: ChatGPT can provide recommendations on cleaning up your system, removing unnecessary files, and optimizing your device's performance.

- System Upgrades: If your system is outdated or struggling with performance issues, ChatGPT can advise on potential upgrades, such as increasing RAM or switching to solid-state drives (SSDs).

5. Data Backup and Recovery

Data is precious, and ChatGPT can assist in ensuring it is safe and recoverable:

- Backup Solutions: ChatGPT can recommend reliable data backup solutions, including cloud services and external storage options, to safeguard your valuable data.

- Data Recovery: In case of data loss, ChatGPT can guide you through data recovery processes, providing steps to retrieve lost files.

Case Study: Resolving a Software Glitch

Let's explore a case study of using ChatGPT to troubleshoot and resolve a software glitch:

Scenario: You're a small business owner experiencing issues with your accounting software.

1. Diagnosing the Problem: You describe the issue to ChatGPT, detailing the symptoms and when they began. ChatGPT asks for information on the software version, operating system, and any recent updates.

2. Troubleshooting Steps: ChatGPT provides a series of troubleshooting steps, including checking for software updates, verifying data integrity, and scanning for conflicting applications.

3. Software Recommendations: After diagnosing the issue as a software conflict, ChatGPT suggests an alternative accounting software solution known for its compatibility with the operating system.

4. Optimization Advice: ChatGPT advises on regular software maintenance and data backup to prevent future issues.

In this case, ChatGPT has guided you through the process of diagnosing and resolving a software glitch in your accounting system, ensuring your business operations can continue smoothly.

Whether you're a tech-savvy individual or someone seeking assistance with technical challenges, ChatGPT is your on-demand support system for troubleshooting and technical problem-solving. With ChatGPT's guidance, you can resolve issues efficiently and maintain the optimal functionality of your digital tools and systems.

5.2 Decision-Making with ChatGPT

Effective decision-making is a critical skill in both personal and professional life. ChatGPT can be a valuable asset when it comes to making informed decisions, offering insights, and assisting in the decision-making process. In this section, we'll explore how ChatGPT can help you make well-informed decisions in a wide range of situations.

1. Gathering Information and Context

The foundation of good decision-making is access to accurate information and a clear understanding of the context. ChatGPT can assist in this crucial first step:

 - Data Analysis: If your decision involves data interpretation, provide the relevant data to ChatGPT. It can help you analyze and draw insights from the data, whether it's financial information, market research, or survey results.

 - Contextual Information: Describe the context of the decision you're facing. ChatGPT can provide background information, historical context, and any relevant factors that might influence the decision.

2. Risk Assessment and Mitigation

Every decision involves an element of risk. ChatGPT can help you assess and manage these risks:

- Risk Analysis: Describe the potential risks associated with your decision. ChatGPT can evaluate these risks and offer strategies to mitigate them, such as risk diversification, contingency planning, or risk-reduction measures.

- Decision Trees: For complex decisions with multiple outcomes, ChatGPT can assist in creating decision trees that map out various scenarios and their associated risks and rewards.

3. Decision-Making Frameworks

ChatGPT can introduce you to established decision-making frameworks that can guide your thinking:

- SWOT Analysis: ChatGPT can help you conduct a SWOT (Strengths, Weaknesses, Opportunities, Threats) analysis to assess the internal and external factors influencing your decision.

- Cost-Benefit Analysis: If your decision involves financial considerations, ChatGPT can guide you through a cost-benefit analysis, helping you weigh the pros and cons and calculate potential returns on investment.

- Ethical Frameworks: In situations involving ethical dilemmas, ChatGPT can introduce ethical frameworks and principles that can inform your decision.

4. Scenario Planning

For complex decisions with uncertain outcomes, scenario planning can be invaluable:

- Scenario Generation: Describe the different scenarios you anticipate, and ChatGPT can help you generate and evaluate potential outcomes for each scenario.

- Contingency Planning: ChatGPT can assist in creating contingency plans for each scenario, ensuring that you're prepared for various outcomes.

5. Decision Optimization

ChatGPT can provide insights on optimizing your decision for the best possible outcome:

- Decision-Making Criteria: Specify the criteria that matter most in your decision. ChatGPT can help you weigh these criteria and provide a scoring system for evaluating options.

- Sensitivity Analysis: If your decision is sensitive to changes in certain variables, ChatGPT can guide you through sensitivity analysis to assess the impact of different variables on your decision.

6. Exploring Alternatives

It's essential to consider a range of alternatives before making a decision. ChatGPT can assist in generating and evaluating alternatives:

- Alternative Generation: Describe the alternatives you've considered, and ChatGPT can propose additional alternatives that you might not have thought of.

- Alternative Evaluation: ChatGPT can help you evaluate each alternative based on your criteria and provide a comparison of their strengths and weaknesses.

Case Study: Making a Strategic Business Decision

Let's examine a case study in which ChatGPT assists in making a strategic business decision:

Scenario: You're a business owner considering whether to expand your product line. You're uncertain about the potential risks and rewards of this decision.

1. Gathering Information: You provide ChatGPT with market research data and your current product line performance. ChatGPT analyzes the data and offers insights into market trends and customer preferences.

2. Risk Assessment: You express concerns about the financial risk of expanding. ChatGPT evaluates the financial risks, suggests risk-reduction strategies, and explores potential sources of revenue.

3. Decision-Making Framework: You request guidance on conducting a cost-benefit analysis for the expansion decision. ChatGPT introduces you to a cost-benefit framework and helps you calculate potential return on investment.

4. Scenario Planning: Worried about uncertain outcomes, you and ChatGPT create scenarios for different market conditions and evaluate the potential impact on the business.

5. Decision Optimization: You define your decision criteria, emphasizing financial stability and growth potential. ChatGPT provides a scoring system to evaluate each alternative product line.

In this case, ChatGPT has been instrumental in guiding you through a complex business decision, offering insights, risk assessment, and structured frameworks for making an informed choice.

Whether you're facing a complex business decision, a personal choice, or an ethical dilemma, ChatGPT can serve as your knowledgeable advisor, providing the information and tools necessary to make well-informed decisions. By harnessing ChatGPT's capabilities, you can navigate the decision-making process with confidence and clarity.

5.3 ChatGPT in Education

The integration of artificial intelligence, such as ChatGPT, into education has transformed the way we learn, teach, and access knowledge. This section explores the myriad ways in which ChatGPT is making a significant impact on education, from personalized learning experiences to assisting educators and students in diverse academic pursuits.

1. Personalized Learning and Homework Assistance

ChatGPT has become an invaluable tool for personalized learning and homework assistance:

- Tutoring and Homework Help: Students can turn to ChatGPT for explanations of difficult concepts, step-by-step guidance on problem-solving, and answers to academic questions across various subjects.

- Adaptive Learning: Educational platforms and institutions integrate ChatGPT to offer adaptive learning experiences. ChatGPT customizes learning paths for students, identifying their strengths and weaknesses to provide tailored instruction.

- Language Learning: ChatGPT can assist language learners by offering conversational practice, language translation, and vocabulary building exercises.

2. Research and Academic Writing

ChatGPT serves as a valuable resource for academic research and writing:

- Research Assistance: Students and researchers can utilize ChatGPT to explore and compile information on a wide range of topics, streamline literature reviews, and generate citations.

- Academic Writing Support: ChatGPT can provide guidance on structuring essays, dissertations, and research papers. It assists in improving writing clarity, coherence, and style.

- Plagiarism Checks: Educational institutions employ ChatGPT for plagiarism detection, ensuring academic integrity.

3. Educational Content Creation

ChatGPT is instrumental in creating educational content for online courses, textbooks, and teaching materials:

- Lesson Planning: Educators can leverage ChatGPT to generate lesson plans, assignments, and assessments aligned with educational standards.

- Textbook Writing: ChatGPT can assist in developing textbooks and instructional content across various subjects.

- Course Development: Educational institutions utilize ChatGPT to build online courses and learning modules, enhancing accessibility and reach.

4. Programming and STEM Education

ChatGPT is a valuable resource for students learning programming and STEM (Science, Technology, Engineering, and Mathematics) subjects:

- Coding Help: Students seeking assistance with coding problems, algorithm design, and debugging can turn to ChatGPT for guidance and code examples.

- STEM Explorations: ChatGPT offers explanations and demonstrations of STEM concepts, making abstract topics more accessible and engaging.

5. Special Education and Inclusivity

ChatGPT plays a role in promoting inclusivity in education:

- Accessibility Features: ChatGPT supports individuals with disabilities by providing alternative formats for educational materials, such as text-to-speech or vice versa.

- Personalized Support: Students with special educational needs benefit from personalized learning experiences, tailored to their unique requirements.

6. Career and College Guidance

ChatGPT aids students in making informed decisions about their career and college choices:

- Career Counseling: ChatGPT can provide insights into various career paths, job market trends, and the skills required for specific professions.

   - College Admissions: ChatGPT offers advice on the college application process, including essay writing, interview preparation, and scholarship opportunities.

7. Language and Cultural Learning

ChatGPT facilitates language learning and cultural understanding:

   - Language Learning: Language learners benefit from immersive conversations with ChatGPT in the target language, improving language skills and cultural awareness.

   - Cultural Insights: ChatGPT provides insights into diverse cultures, customs, and traditions, enhancing global awareness.

Case Study: Personalized Learning in Math

Let's examine a case study demonstrating ChatGPT's role in personalized math learning:

Scenario: A high school student is struggling with understanding complex calculus concepts.

1. Tutoring and Homework Help: The student asks ChatGPT for assistance with a specific calculus problem. ChatGPT provides step-by-step explanations and guides the student to solve the problem independently.

2. Adaptive Learning: The student's school uses an educational platform powered by ChatGPT. The platform analyzes the student's previous test scores and areas of weakness. It then tailors a

personalized calculus learning path, with interactive lessons and quizzes, aimed at reinforcing problem areas.

3. Language Learning: The same student, interested in learning a new language, uses ChatGPT to engage in conversational practice, vocabulary building, and translation exercises.

In this case, ChatGPT has empowered the student to excel in math through personalized learning, while also providing support for language learning.

ChatGPT has emerged as a transformative force in the field of education, enabling personalized learning experiences, assisting in academic research and writing, and promoting inclusivity. Whether you're a student seeking assistance, an educator creating content, or an institution innovating in education, ChatGPT is a versatile tool for enhancing the learning process and advancing academic pursuits.

5.4 Healthcare and Medical Assistance

The integration of AI, such as ChatGPT, into the healthcare industry is revolutionizing the way medical professionals, patients, and caregivers access and manage health information. This section explores the diverse applications of ChatGPT in healthcare and medical assistance, from patient care to medical research.

1. Patient Education and Information

ChatGPT serves as a valuable source of health information for patients and caregivers:

- Symptom Checker: Patients can describe their symptoms to ChatGPT, which can provide initial insights and recommendations, including when to seek medical attention.

- Medical Conditions: ChatGPT offers explanations of various medical conditions, treatment options, and potential outcomes, aiding in patient understanding and decision-making.

- Medication Guidance: ChatGPT can provide information on prescription and over-the-counter medications, including dosage, potential side effects, and interactions.

2. Remote Consultations

Telemedicine has become increasingly popular, and ChatGPT plays a role in remote consultations:

- Virtual Visits: Medical professionals use ChatGPT to conduct virtual appointments, discussing symptoms, offering diagnoses, and providing treatment plans remotely.

- Follow-up Appointments: Patients can engage in follow-up discussions with ChatGPT, addressing treatment progress and any concerns they may have.

3. Healthcare Administration

ChatGPT streamlines administrative tasks within healthcare facilities:

- Appointment Scheduling: Patients can schedule appointments, check availability, and receive reminders via ChatGPT, reducing administrative burden.

- Medical Billing: ChatGPT assists in medical billing processes, helping patients understand their bills and insurance coverage.

- Electronic Health Records (EHR): ChatGPT updates and retrieves EHR data, ensuring that patient records are accurate and easily accessible to medical professionals.

4. Medical Research and Data Analysis

ChatGPT contributes to medical research and data analysis:

- Literature Review: Researchers utilize ChatGPT to conduct comprehensive literature reviews, gathering insights from a vast array of medical journals and studies.

- Data Interpretation: ChatGPT assists in data interpretation, offering insights into research findings and statistical analysis.

- Drug Discovery: ChatGPT accelerates drug discovery by analyzing molecular structures, predicting potential drug candidates, and optimizing chemical formulas.

5. Healthcare Training and Education

ChatGPT enhances medical education:

- Medical School Assistance: Medical students can engage with ChatGPT for explanations of complex medical concepts, assistance with case studies, and preparation for exams.

- Nursing and Allied Health Programs: Nursing students and allied health professionals benefit from ChatGPT's guidance on patient care, treatment procedures, and medical terminology.

6. Mental Health Support

ChatGPT plays a role in mental health support:

- Crisis Intervention: Individuals facing emotional crises can communicate with ChatGPT to receive immediate support and resources.

- Therapy and Coping Strategies: ChatGPT provides guidance on coping strategies, self-help techniques, and mental health resources.

7. Healthcare Policy and Ethical Consultation

ChatGPT assists in healthcare policy and ethical discussions:

- Healthcare Policies: Policymakers engage with ChatGPT to evaluate the potential impact of proposed healthcare policies and regulations.

- Ethical Dilemmas: Medical professionals use ChatGPT to navigate complex ethical dilemmas, such as end-of-life care and organ transplantation.

Case Study: Telemedicine and Remote Consultations

Let's explore a case study demonstrating ChatGPT's role in remote healthcare consultations:

Scenario: A patient is experiencing concerning symptoms and schedules a virtual visit with their primary care physician.

1. Patient Information: The patient provides their symptoms and medical history to ChatGPT. ChatGPT organizes this information for the upcoming virtual appointment.

2. Virtual Consultation: During the virtual consultation, the primary care physician conducts a live video conversation with the patient through a telemedicine platform. ChatGPT assists by displaying relevant medical data and potential diagnoses based on the symptoms.

3. Treatment Plan: The physician and patient discuss the diagnosis and treatment options. ChatGPT generates a summary of the treatment plan, including medication instructions and follow-up appointments.

In this case, ChatGPT has facilitated a seamless remote healthcare consultation, allowing the patient to receive timely medical care and advice without the need for an in-person visit.

ChatGPT is a powerful tool in the healthcare industry, enhancing patient care, supporting medical professionals, aiding in research, and advancing healthcare education. Whether you're a patient seeking medical information or a healthcare professional working to improve patient outcomes, ChatGPT's applications in healthcare are transforming the way we approach medical assistance and support.

CHAPTER VI
Ethics and Responsible Use

6.1 Ensuring Ethical Use of AI

The ethical use of AI, such as ChatGPT, is of paramount importance in our increasingly digital and automated world. This section delves into the core principles, challenges, and strategies for ensuring the responsible and ethical deployment of AI technologies.

1. Core Ethical Principles

To ensure the ethical use of AI, it's essential to adhere to core ethical principles:

  - Transparency: Users and developers should have a clear understanding of how AI systems operate, including their algorithms and data sources.

  - Accountability: There should be accountability for AI decisions. It should be clear who is responsible when AI systems make errors or biased decisions.

  - Privacy: AI systems must respect user privacy. Data should be handled with care and in compliance with relevant data protection regulations.

  - Fairness: AI should be designed and trained to be fair and unbiased, avoiding discrimination based on factors such as race, gender, or socioeconomic status.

2. Identifying and Mitigating Bias

One of the significant challenges in AI ethics is addressing bias in AI systems:

- Data Bias: Data used to train AI systems may contain biases. It's crucial to identify and mitigate these biases to ensure fair and equitable outcomes.

- Algorithmic Bias: The algorithms themselves may introduce bias. Regular auditing and testing are necessary to detect and rectify any discriminatory behavior.

- Fairness Audits: Regular fairness audits can help identify and address potential bias in AI systems, ensuring that they treat all individuals fairly.

3. Informed Consent

In scenarios where AI systems interact with users, informed consent is vital:

- User Awareness: Users should be informed that they are interacting with an AI system. Transparency ensures they understand the nature of the interaction.

- Data Usage: Users should be aware of how their data is collected, stored, and used. Consent should be obtained for data processing.

4. Data Privacy and Security

Data privacy and security are essential aspects of AI ethics:

- Data Encryption: Sensitive data should be encrypted to protect it from unauthorized access and breaches.

- Data Retention Policies: Clear policies on data retention and deletion should be established to ensure that data is not retained longer than necessary.

- Compliance with Regulations: AI systems should adhere to data protection regulations, such as GDPR in Europe or HIPAA in the United States.

5. Combating Misuse

Preventing the misuse of AI is critical for ethical use:

- AI for Harmful Purposes: Developers and users should refrain from using AI for activities that can cause harm, including disinformation campaigns, cyberattacks, or surveillance without consent.

- Ethical Guidelines: Establish ethical guidelines and codes of conduct for AI development and use to prevent misuse.

6. Continuous Monitoring and Improvement

Ensuring ethical AI use is an ongoing process:

- Monitoring and Auditing: Regular monitoring and auditing of AI systems is crucial to identify and rectify any ethical issues that may arise over time.

- Feedback Loops: Implement feedback mechanisms for users and stakeholders to report concerns or bias issues, ensuring that AI systems can be continually improved.

7. Public Awareness and Education

Raising public awareness and educating users about AI ethics is fundamental:

   - Education Programs: Develop educational programs and materials to inform the public about AI ethics, its implications, and responsible use.

   - Ethical AI Design: Encourage the integration of ethics into AI system design and development from the outset.

Case Study: Addressing Bias in AI Customer Service Chatbots

Let's explore a case study of a company committed to addressing bias in their AI-powered customer service chatbot:

Scenario: A company uses an AI chatbot for customer support, but they've received feedback that the chatbot's responses are sometimes biased or offensive.

1. Bias Assessment: The company conducts a thorough assessment of the chatbot's responses and identifies instances of bias, such as gender or racial bias.

2. Bias Mitigation: They retrain the chatbot using a more diverse and inclusive dataset. They also update the algorithm to detect and correct biased responses.

3. Fairness Audits: The company establishes a regular fairness audit process to monitor the chatbot's behavior and ensure it responds fairly to all customers.

4. Transparency and Accountability: They update their chatbot's user interface to clearly indicate when users are interacting with an AI and provide a mechanism for users to report any concerns.

In this case, the company takes proactive steps to ensure that their AI chatbot provides ethical and unbiased customer service, demonstrating their commitment to ethical AI use.

Ethical use of AI is a responsibility shared by developers, users, and policymakers. By adhering to core ethical principles, addressing bias, obtaining informed consent, protecting data privacy and security, and maintaining vigilance through monitoring and education, we can ensure that AI technologies like ChatGPT are used responsibly and ethically, benefiting society as a whole.

6.2 Privacy and Data Security

Privacy and data security are fundamental components of responsible AI use. This section explores the critical aspects of protecting user data and ensuring the security of AI systems, such as ChatGPT.

1. User Data Protection

User data protection is a top priority in AI ethics:

- Data Minimization: AI systems should collect only the data necessary for their intended purpose and avoid excessive data collection.

- User Consent: Users should provide informed consent for data collection and processing. AI systems should clearly explain the purposes for which data is used.

- Anonymization: Whenever possible, data should be anonymized to protect user identities.

- Data Encryption: Data should be encrypted during transmission and storage to prevent unauthorized access.

2. Compliance with Data Regulations

AI systems must adhere to relevant data protection regulations, such as GDPR in Europe or HIPAA in the United States:

- Data Retention: AI systems should follow established data retention policies, which define how long data can be retained and when it must be deleted.

- User Rights: Users should have the right to access their data, request its deletion, and know how their data is being used.

- Data Portability: Users should be able to transfer their data to other services if they wish.

- Data Breach Notification: In the event of a data breach, timely notifications should be provided to affected users and regulatory authorities.

3. Secure Data Handling

AI developers and organizations must ensure secure data handling:

- Data Access Control: Limit access to user data to authorized personnel only. Implement strict access controls to prevent unauthorized data access.

- Data Transmission Security: Ensure that data transmitted between AI systems and users is encrypted, protecting it from interception.

- Data Storage Security: Data should be stored in secure environments with proper safeguards against breaches.

- Data De-Identification: Personal information should be de-identified when not needed for specific tasks.

4. Ethical Data Use

AI should use data ethically and responsibly:

  - Data Purpose Limitation: Use data only for the purposes for which it was collected and avoid using it for unintended or harmful purposes.

  - Avoid Discrimination: AI systems should not use data to discriminate against individuals based on attributes such as race, gender, or age.

5. Transparency

Transparency is essential for user trust:

  - Data Policies: AI systems should provide clear and accessible data policies that explain how user data is handled and used.

  - Data Access Requests: Users should be able to request access to their data and receive understandable explanations of how it is processed.

6. Ongoing Data Security Measures

Data security should be a continuous effort:

- Regular Audits: Conduct regular security audits and assessments to identify and address vulnerabilities.

- Data Backup and Recovery: Implement data backup and recovery procedures to safeguard against data loss.

- Security Training: Ensure that personnel involved in AI development and maintenance receive security training.

Case Study: Securing Healthcare Data with AI

Let's explore a case study where AI is used to secure healthcare data:

Scenario: A healthcare provider uses AI to manage patient records and medical data.

1. Data Encryption: All patient data is stored and transmitted using encryption to prevent unauthorized access.

2. Data Access Control: Access to patient records is restricted to authorized medical personnel, and a strict access control policy is in place.

3. Data De-Identification: Personal information in patient records is de-identified when not required for medical treatment.

4. Regular Audits: The healthcare provider conducts regular security audits to identify vulnerabilities and address them promptly.

5. User Access: Patients can request access to their medical data and receive clear explanations of how it is used and secured.

In this case, the healthcare provider employs AI systems to ensure the privacy and data security of patient records, maintaining the trust of patients and complying with healthcare data regulations.

Protecting user data and ensuring data security are essential aspects of responsible AI use. By adhering to data protection regulations, implementing robust security measures, and maintaining transparency, AI systems like ChatGPT can be used ethically and responsibly while respecting user privacy and data security.

6.3 AI Bias and Fairness

Addressing bias and promoting fairness in AI systems is a critical ethical imperative. This section explores the nuances of AI bias, its consequences, and strategies to ensure fairness in AI, such as ChatGPT.

1. Understanding AI Bias

AI bias refers to systematic and unfair discrimination in the outcomes produced by AI systems. Bias can manifest in various ways, including racial, gender, or socioeconomic bias. It's essential to recognize that bias often arises from biased data, algorithmic decisions, or both.

- Data Bias: Biased training data can perpetuate stereotypes and unfairness. Data may not be representative of the diverse groups AI systems interact with.

- Algorithmic Bias: The design and decision-making processes of AI algorithms can introduce bias. For example, if an algorithm uses biased data to make decisions, it may perpetuate that bias.

2. Consequences of AI Bias

AI bias can have profound real-world consequences:

- Discrimination: AI systems that exhibit bias can discriminate against certain individuals or groups, leading to unfair treatment in areas like employment, lending, or criminal justice.

- Reinforcing Stereotypes: Biased AI systems can perpetuate harmful stereotypes, further entrenching societal inequalities.

- Loss of Trust: Users and stakeholders may lose trust in AI systems that exhibit bias, undermining the technology's credibility.

3. Strategies for Bias Mitigation and Fairness

Ensuring fairness in AI systems is a multifaceted challenge. To mitigate bias and promote fairness, consider the following strategies:

- Diverse and Representative Data: Use diverse and representative training data to reduce bias. Efforts should be made to include data from underrepresented groups.

- Bias Detection Tools: Implement tools and methodologies to detect and measure bias in AI systems. Regular bias audits can help identify and rectify issues.

- Algorithmic Fairness: Research and develop algorithms that prioritize fairness as a core principle, actively working to avoid discriminatory outcomes.

- Human Oversight: Employ human reviewers to assess and moderate AI responses, identifying and addressing biased content.

- Feedback Loops: Establish feedback mechanisms for users and stakeholders to report instances of bias, ensuring continuous improvement.

4. Transparency and Explainability

Transparency is vital in addressing AI bias:

- Explainable AI: Develop AI systems that are explainable, allowing users to understand the rationale behind their decisions.

- Bias Reports: Provide transparency reports that detail efforts to address bias and promote fairness.

5. Ethical Guidelines and Codes of Conduct

Develop and adhere to ethical guidelines and codes of conduct for AI development and use:

- AI Ethics Committees: Establish committees that review and assess the ethical implications of AI systems.

- Public Input: Seek input and feedback from the public and stakeholders to ensure AI systems are developed with diverse perspectives in mind.

6. Continuous Monitoring and Improvement

Bias mitigation is an ongoing process:

- Regular Audits: Conduct regular audits to identify and rectify bias issues that may arise over time.

- Bias Impact Assessments: Assess the real-world impact of AI decisions on individuals and communities to identify and rectify systemic bias.

Case Study: Mitigating Gender Bias in ChatGPT

Let's explore a case study where efforts are made to mitigate gender bias in ChatGPT:

Scenario: Users reported that ChatGPT's responses sometimes exhibited gender bias, such as making stereotypical assumptions about users based on their gender.

1. Bias Detection: The development team implemented a bias detection tool to identify instances of gender bias in ChatGPT's responses.

2. Algorithmic Improvements: The team made algorithmic improvements to avoid making gender-based assumptions and to provide responses that are gender-neutral and respectful.

3. User Feedback Loop: A feedback mechanism was established for users to report instances of gender bias. The team reviewed and addressed reported cases to continually improve the system.

4. Transparency Report: The development team published a transparency report, outlining the steps taken to address gender bias and promoting the principle of fairness in AI.

In this case, the development team actively worked to mitigate gender bias in ChatGPT, striving to provide more inclusive and equitable responses.

Addressing bias and promoting fairness in AI systems is an ongoing journey, but it's essential to make significant strides toward creating AI that respects the dignity and rights of all users, irrespective of their characteristics or backgrounds. By understanding the nature of AI bias, adopting strategies to mitigate it, and prioritizing fairness in AI development, we can create more equitable and unbiased AI systems like ChatGPT.

6.4 Overcoming Challenges and Concerns

The ethical and responsible use of AI, such as ChatGPT, is not without its challenges and concerns. This section addresses key obstacles and provides strategies for addressing them to ensure that AI technologies are used in a way that benefits society.

1. Bias and Fairness Challenges

Challenge: Addressing bias and ensuring fairness in AI systems is an ongoing challenge. Bias can emerge from training data, algorithmic design, and cultural factors.

Solution:

- Diverse Data: Collect and use diverse and representative data for training AI systems to reduce bias and ensure fairness.

- Algorithmic Fairness: Develop and refine algorithms with fairness as a primary goal, actively working to mitigate bias and discrimination.

- Bias Audits: Conduct regular bias audits to identify and rectify instances of bias in AI responses.

2. Privacy and Data Security Concerns

Challenge: Ensuring the privacy and data security of users is a significant concern, especially in an era of increasing data breaches and cyber threats.

Solution:

- Data Encryption: Implement robust data encryption for data transmission and storage to protect it from unauthorized access.

- Compliance with Regulations: Adhere to data protection regulations and establish clear data retention and deletion policies.

- Transparency: Provide users with transparent data policies and data access options to build trust.

3. Accountability and Transparency

Challenge: Determining accountability for AI decisions and ensuring transparency in AI systems can be complex.

Solution:

- Explainable AI: Develop AI systems that are explainable and capable of providing transparent rationales for their decisions.

- Human Oversight: Implement human oversight to assess AI responses, identify issues, and maintain accountability.

- Transparency Reports: Publish transparency reports that detail efforts to address bias, fairness, and accountability.

4. Ethical Education and Awareness

Challenge: Educating the public and AI developers about ethical AI use and its implications is essential but challenging.

Solution:

- AI Ethics Committees: Establish committees to review and assess the ethical implications of AI systems and provide guidance.

- Public Input: Seek input from the public and stakeholders to ensure AI systems are developed with diverse perspectives in mind.

- Educational Programs: Develop educational programs and materials to inform the public about AI ethics and responsible use.

5. Regulatory and Policy Challenges

Challenge: The evolving landscape of AI regulations and policies can be complex and challenging to navigate.

Solution:

- Collaboration: Collaborate with policymakers, legal experts, and regulatory bodies to shape responsible AI policies and regulations.

- Compliance: Stay informed about and comply with evolving AI-related regulations and policies in different regions.

- Ethical Guidelines: Develop and adhere to ethical guidelines and codes of conduct for AI development and use.

6. User Feedback and Continuous Improvement

Challenge: Building mechanisms for user feedback and incorporating it into AI improvements can be a significant challenge.

Solution:

- Feedback Loops: Establish feedback mechanisms for users and stakeholders to report concerns and issues, ensuring continuous improvement.

- Data Impact Assessments: Assess the real-world impact of AI decisions on individuals and communities, identifying and rectifying systemic issues.

- Regular Audits: Conduct regular audits and assessments to identify and address vulnerabilities and concerns.

7. Ethical Case Studies

This section can include ethical case studies that highlight challenges and resolutions in specific scenarios, demonstrating how ethical concerns were overcome and responsible AI use was achieved.

In the ever-evolving landscape of AI, overcoming challenges and addressing concerns is an ongoing endeavor. By actively working to mitigate bias, ensuring privacy and data security, fostering accountability and transparency, promoting ethical education, collaborating with regulators, and maintaining feedback mechanisms, we can navigate the complexities of responsible AI use and build a more ethical and trustworthy AI ecosystem.

CHAPTER VII
Advanced Techniques and Tips

7.1 Fine-Tuning ChatGPT for Specific Tasks

Fine-tuning ChatGPT for specific tasks is a powerful technique that allows you to customize the AI model to excel in a particular domain or application. This section explores the process of fine-tuning, its advantages, and practical tips for achieving optimal results.

1. Understanding Fine-Tuning

Fine-tuning involves training a pre-trained ChatGPT model on a narrower dataset related to your specific task or domain. This process refines the model's capabilities and tailors it to perform well in a particular context. It's essential to understand the following key aspects of fine-tuning:

 - Pre-Trained Model: Start with a pre-trained ChatGPT model, which already possesses a wide range of language skills and knowledge.

 - Domain-Specific Data: Gather or create a dataset that is relevant to your task or industry. This data will be used for fine-tuning.

 - Task-Specific Objectives: Define clear objectives for your task and how you want the model to perform. For example, if you're fine-tuning for medical diagnosis, specify the criteria for accurate diagnoses.

- Fine-Tuning Process: Fine-tuning typically involves several training iterations to optimize the model's performance.

2. Advantages of Fine-Tuning

Fine-tuning offers several advantages for specific tasks:

- Improved Task Performance: Fine-tuned models are better equipped to provide accurate and contextually relevant responses for a specific domain.

- Domain Expertise: The model gains domain-specific knowledge and can understand and generate content that aligns with your task.

- Efficiency: Fine-tuned models often require fewer training steps and less data compared to training a model from scratch.

3. Steps for Fine-Tuning

Fine-tuning ChatGPT for specific tasks involves a series of steps:

- Data Collection: Gather or create a dataset that is representative of your task or domain. Ensure that it covers various scenarios and use cases.

- Preprocessing: Clean and preprocess the data to ensure it's suitable for fine-tuning. This may include text normalization, removing duplicates, and data augmentation.

- Fine-Tuning: Use specialized training processes to fine-tune the model on your dataset. This may involve transfer learning techniques where you leverage the pre-trained model's knowledge.

- Hyperparameter Tuning: Experiment with different hyperparameters to optimize the model's performance. This includes batch size, learning rate, and the number of training iterations.

- Validation: Use a separate validation dataset to assess the model's performance during fine-tuning. Make necessary adjustments based on validation results.

4. Fine-Tuning Best Practices

To achieve the best results when fine-tuning ChatGPT, consider the following best practices:

- Diverse Data: Ensure that your training data represents the full range of scenarios and variations in your specific task.

- Regular Updates: Fine-tuned models may require periodic updates as your task evolves or new data becomes available.

- Ethical Considerations: Be aware of ethical considerations when fine-tuning, such as avoiding bias and ensuring data privacy.

- Monitoring and Evaluation: Continuously monitor the model's performance and seek user feedback to further improve its responses.

5. Fine-Tuning Use Cases

Fine-tuning ChatGPT has a wide range of practical applications, such as:

- Customer Support: Tailoring ChatGPT for providing customer support in various industries, addressing specific customer queries effectively.

- Medical Diagnosis: Fine-tuning for medical professionals to assist in diagnosing illnesses and suggesting treatment options.

- Legal Services: Customizing ChatGPT to provide legal advice and assistance in legal research.

- Content Generation: Fine-tuning for content creation, such as generating marketing copy, technical documentation, or creative writing.

- Financial Analysis: Adapting ChatGPT for financial institutions to provide insights into market trends, investment strategies, and risk assessments.

Fine-tuning ChatGPT for specific tasks empowers organizations to leverage the AI model's capabilities to their advantage, making it a valuable asset in various industries and applications. By following best practices, continuously monitoring performance, and staying attentive to ethical considerations, you can harness the power of fine-tuned ChatGPT to achieve outstanding results in your specific domain or task.

7.2 Integration with Other Tools and Services

Integrating ChatGPT with various tools and services can greatly enhance its functionality and provide tailored solutions for specific tasks and industries. This section explores the methods, benefits, and practical considerations for integrating ChatGPT with external tools and services.

1. Understanding Integration

Integration involves connecting ChatGPT with external software, applications, or services to expand its capabilities and create a more holistic AI-powered solution. This integration can take various forms, such as API connections, plugins, or custom interfaces.

 - API Integration: ChatGPT can be accessed through an API (Application Programming Interface) that allows developers to interact with it programmatically.

 - Plugin Integration: Integrate ChatGPT as a plugin within existing software applications, making it accessible to users directly.

 - Custom Interfaces: Create custom interfaces or chatbots that use ChatGPT as a component to provide tailored solutions.

2. Benefits of Integration

Integrating ChatGPT with other tools and services offers several advantages:

- Enhanced Functionality: Combining ChatGPT with specific tools can extend its functionality, enabling it to perform tasks that go beyond general conversation.

- Industry Adaptation: Integration allows ChatGPT to adapt to various industries and domains, making it a versatile tool for diverse applications.

- Workflow Automation: Integration can automate routine tasks, streamline workflows, and provide quick access to information or insights.

3. Integration Use Cases

Consider the following use cases for integrating ChatGPT with external tools and services:

- Customer Support Chatbots: Integrate ChatGPT into customer support chatbots to provide intelligent responses and assist customers with inquiries.

- Content Generation Tools: Combine ChatGPT with content generation tools to streamline the process of creating marketing materials, articles, or reports.

- Data Analysis Platforms: Integrate ChatGPT with data analysis platforms to obtain insights and explanations for complex datasets.

- E-commerce Assistants: Create e-commerce assistants that use ChatGPT to answer customer queries and provide product recommendations.

- Healthcare Decision Support: Integrate ChatGPT with healthcare systems to assist medical professionals in making clinical decisions.

4. Practical Considerations

Successful integration requires attention to practical considerations:

- Data Security: Ensure that data shared between ChatGPT and external tools is secure and complies with data protection regulations.

- Scalability: Consider how the integration will scale with growing user demands and usage.

- Customization: Tailor the integration to specific use cases and industry requirements, adjusting parameters and configurations as needed.

- User Experience: Prioritize user experience by creating seamless interactions between ChatGPT and other tools.

5. API Integration

API integration is a common method for connecting ChatGPT with other tools and services:

- API Access: ChatGPT providers often offer API access, allowing developers to interact with the model programmatically.

- Authentication: Implement secure authentication methods to ensure that only authorized users or applications can access ChatGPT through the API.

- Response Handling: Develop systems to handle and parse responses from the ChatGPT API, presenting them in a user-friendly manner.

6. Plugin Integration

For plugin integration, consider the following:

- Plugin Development: Develop plugins that seamlessly incorporate ChatGPT within existing software applications.

- User Interface: Ensure that the user interface is intuitive and integrates ChatGPT's capabilities seamlessly.

7. Case Study: ChatGPT in Customer Support

Let's explore a case study where ChatGPT is integrated into a customer support system:

Scenario: An e-commerce company integrates ChatGPT into its customer support chat system.

1. API Integration: The company accesses ChatGPT via its API, which allows real-time communication.

2. Authentication: Secure authentication methods are implemented to ensure that only authorized customer support agents can use ChatGPT.

3. User-Friendly Interface: The integration features a user-friendly interface that allows agents to easily interact with ChatGPT and retrieve responses to assist customers.

In this case, ChatGPT integration enhances the customer support system's capabilities, providing customers with intelligent responses and support agents with valuable information to assist customers more effectively.

Integrating ChatGPT with external tools and services unlocks a world of possibilities, making it a versatile tool for numerous industries and applications. By understanding the integration methods, benefits, and use cases, and paying attention to practical considerations, organizations can create more powerful, efficient, and customized solutions that leverage the capabilities of ChatGPT to their advantage.

7.3 ChatGPT in Business and Industry

ChatGPT has emerged as a transformative tool with a wide range of applications across various sectors. This section delves into the specific ways in which ChatGPT is leveraged to drive innovation, streamline operations, and enhance customer experiences in business and industry.

1. Customer Support and Engagement

Scenario: Many businesses are using ChatGPT to enhance customer support and engagement. Here's how it works:

 - Live Chat Assistance: Businesses integrate ChatGPT into their websites and chat platforms to provide real-time assistance to customers. Customers can get immediate answers to queries or assistance with product selection.

 - Efficient Ticket Resolution: ChatGPT can be used to streamline the resolution of customer support tickets. By automatically categorizing and responding to common issues, it frees up support agents to focus on more complex problems.

 - Personalized Recommendations: ChatGPT analyzes customer data to provide personalized product recommendations. For e-commerce, this results in higher sales and improved customer satisfaction.

2. Content Generation and Marketing

Scenario: In content generation and marketing, ChatGPT is a valuable asset. Here's how it's utilized:

- Automated Content Creation: ChatGPT can generate high-quality content, such as blog posts, social media updates, and product descriptions. This saves businesses time and resources while maintaining consistency and quality.

- A/B Testing Suggestions: ChatGPT can provide suggestions for A/B testing, helping marketers optimize their campaigns for better performance.

- Content Calendar Planning: Businesses use ChatGPT to assist in content calendar planning. It can suggest topics, keywords, and publication schedules based on trending topics and user preferences.

3. Data Analysis and Insights

Scenario: Industries rely on ChatGPT to derive insights from data and improve decision-making processes:

- Data Interpretation: ChatGPT is applied to analyze and interpret data sets, making it easier for businesses to understand trends, identify opportunities, and make data-driven decisions.

- Market Research: It assists in market research by processing vast amounts of unstructured data from sources like social media, reviews, and news articles to uncover market trends and customer sentiments.

- Financial Analysis: In finance, ChatGPT aids in analyzing market data and financial reports, providing insights for investment decisions and risk assessments.

4. Workflow Automation

Scenario: Workflow automation is a key area where ChatGPT is employed for increased efficiency:

- Administrative Tasks: ChatGPT automates various administrative tasks such as scheduling, data entry, and report generation, freeing up employees for more strategic work.

- Customer Onboarding: It streamlines customer onboarding processes by guiding customers through setup procedures and answering common queries.

- Document Summarization: Businesses use ChatGPT to summarize lengthy documents, reducing the time spent on reading and analyzing reports.

5. Personalized Marketing and Sales

Scenario: Personalized marketing and sales are enhanced with ChatGPT:

- Lead Qualification: ChatGPT assists sales teams by qualifying leads based on interaction data and providing insights into lead behavior and potential conversion.

- Product Recommendations: E-commerce sites employ ChatGPT to deliver personalized product recommendations, increasing cross-selling and upselling opportunities.

- Email Marketing: ChatGPT generates personalized email marketing content that resonates with individual customers, leading to higher engagement and conversion rates.

6. Industry-Specific Applications

ChatGPT finds application in various industries:

- Healthcare: It offers diagnostic support, drug information, and patient interaction in healthcare, improving the quality of care.

- Legal Services: Legal professionals leverage ChatGPT for legal research, contract analysis, and generating legal documents.

- Manufacturing: In manufacturing, ChatGPT assists in process optimization, quality control, and supply chain management.

- Education: ChatGPT aids educators in creating educational content, answering student queries, and offering personalized learning experiences.

7. Challenges and Considerations

While ChatGPT offers numerous benefits, businesses must also consider challenges, including ethical use, data privacy, and bias. Ethical guidelines and responsible use of ChatGPT are essential to maintain trust and fairness in interactions.

8. Case Study: ChatGPT in E-commerce

Let's explore a case study illustrating how ChatGPT is applied in the e-commerce industry:

Scenario: An e-commerce company employs ChatGPT for customer support, content generation, and personalized marketing.

1. Customer Support: ChatGPT assists customers by providing instant responses to queries, improving response time, and enhancing customer satisfaction.

2. Content Generation: The company uses ChatGPT to generate product descriptions, blog posts, and social media content, saving time and maintaining consistency.

3. Personalized Marketing: ChatGPT analyzes customer behavior and provides product recommendations, resulting in increased sales and customer engagement.

ChatGPT has significantly enhanced the company's operations, contributing to increased sales and customer satisfaction.

ChatGPT's application in business and industry showcases its adaptability and potential for improving efficiency, customer experiences, and decision-making processes. By recognizing the specific advantages and challenges, industries can harness the capabilities of ChatGPT to remain competitive and innovative in today's fast-paced business landscape.

7.4 Future Possibilities and Trends

As ChatGPT continues to evolve and demonstrate its capabilities, it opens up a world of exciting possibilities and trends that have the potential to reshape various industries and sectors. This section explores the future directions and emerging trends for ChatGPT and AI-powered technologies.

1. Multimodal Capabilities

Future iterations of ChatGPT are likely to incorporate multimodal capabilities, enabling the model to understand and generate content beyond text. This means ChatGPT can interpret and generate images, videos, and text simultaneously, making it a versatile tool for a wide range of applications.

  - Content Generation: ChatGPT can create multimedia content, including interactive presentations, educational videos, and visual storytelling.

  - Visual Assistants: It can serve as a visual assistant for tasks like image and video editing, providing real-time suggestions and enhancements.

2. Improved Contextual Understanding

ChatGPT's ability to understand context is expected to improve significantly. This means the model can carry more extended conversations, understand nuanced topics, and maintain context over multiple interactions.

  - Long-Form Content: ChatGPT can assist in writing long-form content like novels, research papers, and reports by maintaining a consistent writing style and flow.

- Advanced Personalization: It can offer highly personalized recommendations and responses, enhancing user experiences.

3. Industry-Specific Customization

Industries will continue to customize ChatGPT for specific use cases. Companies will fine-tune the model to excel in their respective domains, further expanding its adoption in sectors such as finance, healthcare, legal services, and more.

- Specialized Assistants: Industry-specific ChatGPT variants will serve as virtual assistants for professionals, aiding in complex tasks and decision-making.

- Domain Expertise: ChatGPT will possess deep domain knowledge, becoming a valuable resource for professionals in various fields.

4. Ethical AI and Fairness

The future of ChatGPT will place a stronger emphasis on ethical considerations and fairness. Developers and organizations will invest in technologies and practices to minimize biases and ensure responsible AI use.

- Bias Mitigation: Ongoing efforts to reduce biases in AI will result in fairer and more inclusive interactions.

- Data Privacy: Enhanced data privacy measures will protect user information and build trust in AI applications.

5. Real-World Applications

ChatGPT and similar models will be further integrated into real-world applications, enhancing efficiency, productivity, and user experiences across various sectors.

- Education: ChatGPT will play a pivotal role in personalized education, assisting students with their learning needs and providing virtual tutors.

- Telemedicine: It will provide advanced medical advice, diagnosis, and treatment recommendations, extending healthcare access globally.

- Innovation Acceleration: ChatGPT will contribute to accelerating innovation by aiding in research, ideation, and problem-solving.

6. ChatGPT for Creativity and Art

The creative potential of ChatGPT will be explored further, leading to innovations in art, music, and design.

- Artistic Collaboration: ChatGPT can collaborate with artists to generate artworks, music compositions, and design concepts.

- Storytelling: It can assist in co-authoring novels, scripts, and interactive storytelling experiences.

7. Multilingual and Global Accessibility

ChatGPT will continue to expand its multilingual capabilities, making it accessible to a more diverse global audience.

- Language Support: It will provide support for a broader range of languages, fostering global communication.

- Cultural Sensitivity: Efforts will be made to ensure cultural sensitivity in responses, enhancing cross-cultural interactions.

8. Integration with Everyday Life

ChatGPT will seamlessly integrate into people's daily lives, becoming an essential tool for tasks, creativity, learning, and communication.

- Voice Interfaces: It will interact through voice interfaces, offering assistance in everyday tasks and conversations.

- Personal Assistant: ChatGPT will serve as a reliable personal assistant for organizing schedules, providing recommendations, and answering questions.

9. The Role of Regulation and Policy

The development and deployment of ChatGPT will continue to be guided by regulations and policies to ensure responsible and ethical use. Governments and organizations will collaborate to establish frameworks for AI governance.

- Transparency: Regulations will promote transparency in AI decision-making processes and the use of AI in various industries.

- Accountability: Policies will hold developers and organizations accountable for the ethical use of AI.

The future of ChatGPT is filled with incredible possibilities and trends that will reshape industries, enhance user experiences, and drive innovation. While these advancements hold great promise, they also come with the responsibility of ensuring ethical and responsible AI use, guided by regulations and policies that prioritize fairness, transparency, and data privacy. As ChatGPT continues to evolve, it will serve as a valuable tool in a rapidly changing technological landscape.

CHAPTER VIII
User Stories

8.1 Real-Life Success Stories

The real-life success stories of individuals and organizations that have harnessed the power of ChatGPT serve as powerful testaments to the transformative potential of AI. In this section, we explore specific cases where ChatGPT has made a significant impact, driving innovation and achieving remarkable outcomes.

1. Streamlining Customer Support with ChatGPT

Case Study: Tech Support Company

A tech support company integrated ChatGPT into its customer support platform, aiming to reduce response times and enhance customer satisfaction. The results were astonishing:

- Response Time Reduction: ChatGPT's instant response capabilities led to a 40% reduction in response times. Customers received quick solutions to their queries, resulting in higher satisfaction rates.

- 24/7 Support: With ChatGPT's availability round the clock, the company was able to offer 24/7 customer support without the need to hire additional staff.

- Scalability: As the company grew, ChatGPT seamlessly scaled to accommodate increased customer interactions without compromising quality.

2. Accelerating Research in Healthcare

Case Study: Medical Research Institution

A renowned medical research institution incorporated ChatGPT into its research process. By feeding ChatGPT a wide range of medical data, the institution achieved groundbreaking results:

- Rapid Literature Review: ChatGPT conducted literature reviews in a fraction of the time it would have taken human researchers. This accelerated the institution's ability to stay updated with the latest medical studies.

- Data Interpretation: ChatGPT aided in interpreting complex medical datasets, helping researchers identify patterns, potential treatments, and new research directions.

- Publication Assistance: Research papers and articles co-authored with ChatGPT received widespread recognition and were published in prestigious medical journals.

3. Enhancing Creativity in Design

Case Study: Design Agency

A design agency collaborated with ChatGPT to enhance their creative processes. The results were remarkable:

- Idea Generation: ChatGPT assisted in brainstorming sessions, generating unique design ideas and concepts that provided a fresh perspective for the agency's projects.

- Design Concepts: The agency utilized ChatGPT to create initial design concepts for clients, saving time and resources.

- Efficiency Gains: With ChatGPT's assistance, the agency increased its project turnover rate, satisfying more clients and expanding its portfolio.

4. Personalized Learning in Education

Case Study: Educational Institution

An educational institution introduced ChatGPT to personalize the learning experience for students. The outcomes were transformative:

- Individualized Lessons: ChatGPT developed customized learning paths for each student, addressing their specific strengths and weaknesses.

- Homework and Assessment: Students received instant feedback on assignments and assessments, leading to improved academic performance.

- Student Engagement: With interactive lessons and Q&A sessions facilitated by ChatGPT, student engagement and enthusiasm for learning significantly increased.

5. Empowering Small Businesses

Case Study: Small Retailers

Small retailers harnessed ChatGPT's capabilities to compete with larger e-commerce platforms:

- Content Creation: ChatGPT generated product descriptions, blog posts, and marketing content, enabling small retailers to maintain a professional online presence.

- Customer Engagement: Real-time customer support chatbots powered by ChatGPT offered a personalized shopping experience, rivaling that of larger competitors.

- Market Insights: Small retailers used ChatGPT to analyze market trends and customer sentiments, allowing them to make informed business decisions.

These real-life success stories exemplify the remarkable impact of ChatGPT across various domains. They showcase how individuals and organizations have harnessed its capabilities to streamline operations, drive innovation, and achieve remarkable outcomes, all while enhancing customer satisfaction and user experiences. As these stories continue to unfold, they offer a glimpse into the boundless potential of AI in shaping our future.

8.2 User Experiences with ChatGPT

The adoption of ChatGPT has led to a myriad of unique and insightful user experiences. In this section, we'll delve into specific anecdotes and accounts from users who have interacted with ChatGPT, highlighting the impact it has had on their lives, businesses, and daily routines.

1. Empowering Entrepreneurs and Small Business Owners

Entrepreneurs and small business owners have found ChatGPT to be a game-changer, offering innovative solutions and cost-effective tools that level the playing field against larger competitors:

- Content Generation: Entrepreneurs leverage ChatGPT to create engaging and professional content, whether it's for websites, marketing materials, or social media. This not only saves them time but also ensures their online presence is as polished as that of established businesses.

- Customer Engagement: Small businesses use ChatGPT to provide efficient and personalized customer support through chatbots. This results in enhanced customer engagement and fosters loyalty, as customers appreciate the quick and accurate responses.

- Market Analysis: Entrepreneurs use ChatGPT to gather and analyze market data, enabling them to make informed decisions about their product offerings, target audiences, and pricing strategies.

2. Revolutionizing Healthcare and Telemedicine

The healthcare sector has witnessed a profound transformation with the introduction of ChatGPT. Patients and healthcare professionals alike have shared their experiences:

- Patient Support: Patients utilize ChatGPT for initial health queries and to understand symptoms. This accessibility to medical information has been a valuable resource for individuals looking for guidance and reassurance.

- Diagnostic Assistance: Healthcare practitioners integrate ChatGPT into their diagnostic processes. By inputting patient symptoms, the model aids in narrowing down potential conditions and provides recommendations for further medical assessments.

- Telemedicine: Telemedicine services use ChatGPT for remote patient consultations. The model assists in capturing patient history and presenting preliminary diagnosis, facilitating efficient telehealth visits.

3. Academic Advancements in Education

Educators and students have harnessed ChatGPT's capabilities to improve academic outcomes and make learning more engaging:

- Homework Help: Students turn to ChatGPT for assistance with homework and assignments. The model provides explanations, solutions, and guidance on complex problems, boosting student performance.

- Interactive Learning: Educators use ChatGPT to create interactive lessons and quizzes. This dynamic learning experience enhances student engagement and facilitates self-paced learning.

- Language Learning: Language learners have experienced immersive language practice by conversing with ChatGPT in their target language, improving their speaking and comprehension skills.

4. Personal Creative Collaborations

ChatGPT has become a creative collaborator for artists, writers, and designers, enhancing their creative processes:

- Artistic Collaboration: Artists collaborate with ChatGPT to generate novel ideas for art projects. The model provides inspiration, suggestions, and even contributes to the artwork itself.

- Creative Writing: Writers co-author stories, poems, and novels with ChatGPT. The model's ability to generate text and ideas sparks creativity and leads to innovative storytelling.

- Design Inspiration: Designers receive design suggestions and concepts from ChatGPT, streamlining their creative workflow and pushing the boundaries of their artistic endeavors.

5. Cross-Cultural Communication

ChatGPT's multilingual capabilities have facilitated cross-cultural exchanges and enhanced global communication:

- Language Learning: Language enthusiasts use ChatGPT for language practice and learning. The model's understanding of various languages and cultures enriches language acquisition experiences.

- Global Business: Multinational companies use ChatGPT to communicate with customers and partners across different regions. The model's multilingual support fosters international business interactions.

- Cultural Sensitivity: Users appreciate ChatGPT's efforts to provide culturally sensitive responses, ensuring respectful and inclusive cross-cultural dialogues.

These user experiences with ChatGPT highlight the model's versatility and its profound impact on various aspects of our lives. From empowering entrepreneurs to revolutionizing healthcare and education, and facilitating cross-cultural communication, ChatGPT has touched the lives of countless individuals, businesses, and communities, shaping the way we work, learn, and communicate in the digital age.

8.3 Lessons Learned

The journey of integrating ChatGPT into various aspects of our lives and work has been enlightening, revealing valuable lessons that have shaped the responsible use of AI. In this section, we'll explore some of the key lessons learned from the user experiences, challenges, and successes with ChatGPT.

1. Ethical Considerations and Bias Mitigation

As ChatGPT's capabilities expanded, the importance of ethical considerations and bias mitigation became apparent. Lessons learned in this regard include:

- Training Data Diversity: Ensuring diverse and representative training data is crucial to minimize biases in responses and recommendations.

- Ongoing Monitoring: Continuous monitoring of interactions and feedback mechanisms is necessary to identify and rectify potential biases or ethical concerns.

- User Education: Users must be educated on the capabilities and limitations of AI to foster responsible and ethical use.

2. Data Privacy and Security

The use of AI, including ChatGPT, highlighted the significance of data privacy and security:

- Data Encryption: Lessons emphasized the need for strong data encryption methods to protect sensitive information when interacting with AI models.

- Consent and Transparency: Users expect transparency about data usage and require the option to provide or withhold consent for data collection.

- Data Retention Policies: Establishing clear data retention policies and allowing users to control their data's lifespan are integral to maintaining trust.

3. User Training and Proficiency

Users learned that proficiency with ChatGPT enhances the quality of interactions:

- Effective Querying: Users who were proficient in formulating queries and providing context received more accurate and valuable responses.

- Interacting with Boundaries: Understanding the model's limitations helped users make the most of their interactions without expecting AI to replace human expertise entirely.

- Feedback Loop: Implementing feedback mechanisms allowed users to train and fine-tune ChatGPT for specific tasks, improving its performance.

4. Collaborative Potential

Users discovered the collaborative potential of ChatGPT:

- Human-AI Collaboration: Collaborative projects involving humans and ChatGPT led to innovative solutions and creative outcomes that neither party could achieve alone.

- Teamwork and Ideation: ChatGPT became a valuable team member, facilitating brainstorming, idea generation, and project development.

- Feedback Loop: Encouraging user feedback helped developers and organizations improve the model's capabilities, benefiting the entire user community.

5. Human-AI Balance

Maintaining a healthy balance between human expertise and AI assistance was a critical lesson:

- Complementary Role: Users realized that ChatGPT is most effective when it complements human skills, rather than attempting to replace them entirely.

- Guidance, Not Decisions: ChatGPT can guide decision-making, but final decisions should be made by humans who consider ethical, legal, and subjective factors.

- Human Oversight: Users recognized the need for human oversight to ensure AI recommendations align with their goals and values.

6. Adaptability and Integration

Flexibility and adaptability are essential lessons when integrating ChatGPT into workflows:

- Customization: Organizations learned to fine-tune ChatGPT to suit specific tasks, industries, and contexts.

- Integration: Seamlessly integrating ChatGPT with existing tools and services enhanced efficiency and productivity.

- Scalability: The adaptability of ChatGPT allowed for scalability as user demands increased.

These lessons learned underscore the dynamic and evolving nature of AI integration into our lives and work. As ChatGPT continues to advance and find its place in various industries, the experiences and insights gained will be invaluable in shaping a future where AI collaborates with humans to drive innovation, productivity, and ethical use.

Appendix

Glossary of ChatGPT Terms

Understanding the terminology associated with ChatGPT is essential for effective use and communication. This glossary provides clear and concise definitions of key terms related to ChatGPT and AI.

1. ChatGPT: A state-of-the-art language model developed by OpenAI, capable of understanding and generating human-like text, making it a versatile tool for various applications.

2. AI (Artificial Intelligence): The simulation of human intelligence processes by machines, including learning, reasoning, problem-solving, perception, and language understanding.

3. NLP (Natural Language Processing): A field of AI focused on the interaction between computers and human language, enabling machines to understand, interpret, and generate text.

4. Language Model: A statistical model that is trained to predict the probability of a word or sequence of words based on the context of the language.

5. Fine-Tuning: The process of adapting a pre-trained language model, like ChatGPT, to perform specific tasks or generate desired responses.

6. Chatbot: A computer program designed to simulate conversation with human users, often used for customer support, information retrieval, or entertainment.

7. Response Generation: The ability of ChatGPT to produce coherent and contextually relevant text in response to user queries or prompts.

8. Data Training: The process of providing large amounts of text data to train a language model like ChatGPT, allowing it to learn patterns and language understanding.

9. Prompt: A user-provided input or query given to ChatGPT to initiate a conversation or request a specific response.

10. Context: The text or information provided to ChatGPT that informs its responses and ensures continuity in a conversation.

11. Bias: In the context of AI, bias refers to the presence of unfair or skewed patterns in the responses generated by the model, often influenced by the data used for training.

12. Ethical Use: The responsible and fair use of AI and ChatGPT, considering the potential impacts on individuals and society, and avoiding harmful or discriminatory behavior.

13. Data Privacy: The protection of user data and information when interacting with AI models like ChatGPT, including measures to prevent unauthorized access.

14. Human Oversight: The practice of having humans review and supervise AI-generated content to ensure it aligns with ethical and quality standards.

15. Bias Mitigation: Strategies and techniques employed to reduce or eliminate bias in AI responses, promoting fairness and equity.

16. User Proficiency: The user's level of skill and understanding in formulating queries and providing context for effective interactions with ChatGPT.

17. Feedback Loop: A mechanism for users to provide feedback on AI responses, which can be used to improve and fine-tune the model.

18. Customization: The process of modifying ChatGPT to suit specific tasks, industries, or use cases, enhancing its performance and relevance.

19. Integration: The seamless incorporation of ChatGPT into existing tools, platforms, or workflows, ensuring compatibility and efficiency.

20. Scalability: The ability of ChatGPT to handle increased workloads and user interactions without compromising performance.

This glossary serves as a valuable reference to demystify the language of ChatGPT and AI, empowering users to engage effectively with the technology and make informed decisions about its applications. Understanding these terms is essential for harnessing the full potential of ChatGPT and ensuring responsible and ethical use.

Frequently Asked Questions

In this section, we address common questions and concerns that users often have about ChatGPT, offering clear and informative answers to help you navigate your AI journey effectively.

1. What is ChatGPT, and how does it work?

   - ChatGPT is an AI language model developed by OpenAI. It works by using deep learning techniques to understand and generate human-like text based on the context provided in user queries or prompts. It has been trained on a large corpus of text data to predict and generate coherent responses.

2. What can I use ChatGPT for?

   - ChatGPT is a versatile tool with a wide range of applications. You can use it for content generation, research assistance, data analysis, brainstorming, creative writing, decision-making support, and much more. Its flexibility makes it suitable for various industries and use cases.

3. Is ChatGPT capable of understanding specific domains or industries?

   - ChatGPT can be fine-tuned to understand and generate text related to specific domains or industries. Fine-tuning allows you to customize the model for tasks such as medical research, legal documents, or technical support, making it more domain-specific.

4. What are some ethical considerations when using ChatGPT?

- Ethical use is crucial. Consider the potential for biases in AI-generated content, protect user data and privacy, and implement human oversight to ensure responsible use. OpenAI provides guidelines for ethical AI use that you should follow.

5. How can I improve the quality of responses from ChatGPT?

- Providing clear and detailed prompts or queries is essential. Users who are proficient in formulating questions and offering context tend to receive more accurate and valuable responses. A feedback loop can also help improve ChatGPT's performance.

6. Is ChatGPT suitable for business and industry use?

- Yes, ChatGPT is increasingly being adopted by businesses for tasks such as customer support, content generation, and data analysis. Its adaptability and integration capabilities make it a valuable tool in various industries.

7. How do I ensure data privacy when using ChatGPT?

- Implement strong data encryption measures, establish clear data retention policies, and provide transparency to users regarding data usage. Always prioritize data security to protect sensitive information.

8. What are some potential future trends in AI and ChatGPT?

- Future possibilities include AI models becoming more specialized and tailored to specific tasks, improved understanding of context and user intent, and enhanced collaboration between humans and AI. AI is expected to play a more significant role in various industries.

9. How do I report issues or provide feedback on ChatGPT?

- OpenAI encourages users to provide feedback on problematic model outputs through the provided interfaces. Your feedback can help improve the model's performance and ensure responsible use.

10. Where can I find more technical documentation and resources about ChatGPT?

- OpenAI's official documentation, including API documentation and guidelines, is available for technical users. Additionally, academic journals, research papers, and online communities are valuable resources for in-depth information.

These frequently asked questions provide essential insights into ChatGPT and its various aspects. Understanding these key points will help you make informed decisions about the responsible and effective use of AI in your projects and endeavors.

Conclusion

Harnessing the Power of ChatGPT

As we near the end of this journey exploring the incredible capabilities of ChatGPT, it's essential to understand how to harness its power effectively. ChatGPT has the potential to be a game-changer in various aspects of our lives, whether in business, education, research, or personal productivity. In this section, we'll delve into specific strategies and best practices for maximizing the benefits of ChatGPT while ensuring ethical and responsible use.

1. Clarifying Your Objectives

Before fully embracing ChatGPT, it's crucial to define your objectives clearly. What specific tasks or challenges are you looking to address with AI assistance? Whether it's content generation, data analysis, or creative writing, having a well-defined purpose will guide your interactions with ChatGPT and help you achieve meaningful outcomes.

2. Crafting Effective Prompts

One of the key determinants of ChatGPT's performance is the quality of the prompts or queries you provide. To get the most accurate and valuable responses, it's essential to be proficient in crafting clear, context-rich queries. This proficiency comes with practice, as you learn to structure questions effectively, provide relevant context, and iterate on your queries to refine the results.

3. Iterative Learning

Using ChatGPT is not a one-and-done process; it's an ongoing journey of learning and improvement. It's advisable to adopt an iterative approach where you continuously refine your queries, experiment with different phrasings, and use user feedback to enhance the model's performance. Over time, you'll develop a deeper understanding of how to extract the information you need effectively.

4. Human Oversight and Feedback

Maintaining a human-in-the-loop approach is essential, especially in high-stakes applications. Regularly review the AI-generated content to ensure accuracy and relevance. Establish feedback loops to report issues or areas for improvement to the development team. Human oversight is a crucial element in ensuring responsible and ethical AI use.

5. Customization and Fine-Tuning

ChatGPT's adaptability makes it a powerful tool. Consider fine-tuning the model for specific tasks or industries to maximize its relevance and accuracy. This process allows you to customize ChatGPT's responses, making it even more valuable in niche applications.

6. Data Privacy and Security

When dealing with sensitive information, data privacy and security should be paramount. Implement robust data encryption measures and follow data protection regulations to ensure the confidentiality of user information. Transparency about data usage is essential for building trust.

7. Scalability and Integration

As your use of ChatGPT grows, you'll need to consider scalability and integration. Ensure that ChatGPT can handle increased workloads and seamlessly integrate with your existing tools and services. Adaptability and scalability will be key in realizing the full potential of ChatGPT within your workflow.

8. Ethical Use and Bias Mitigation

Always be vigilant about the ethical use of AI. Avoid biased or discriminatory content and adopt strategies to mitigate bias. OpenAI's guidelines on AI ethics and bias mitigation should be closely followed to ensure responsible use.

9. Collaborative Human-AI Future

Looking ahead, the future of AI assistance holds the promise of a collaborative partnership between humans and machines. Embracing ChatGPT is a step toward that future. As AI continues to evolve and become more specialized, it will work alongside us, enhancing our capabilities and enabling us to tackle complex challenges more effectively.

By following these strategies and best practices, you'll be well-equipped to harness the full power of ChatGPT. As AI assistance becomes increasingly integral to our lives, responsible and effective utilization will be the key to success in both personal and professional endeavors. With ChatGPT at your side, you have a powerful tool to unlock new possibilities and achieve your goals.

Looking Ahead: The Future of AI Assistance

As we conclude our exploration of ChatGPT's remarkable capabilities and its impact on various aspects of our lives, it's crucial to turn our attention to the exciting possibilities and trends that lie ahead in the realm of AI assistance. The future of AI assistance promises to be dynamic, transformative, and filled with opportunities to enhance our personal and professional lives. In this section, we will dive into specific trends and potential developments that will shape the future landscape of AI assistance.

1. Specialization and Domain Expertise

One of the key trends on the horizon is the growing specialization of AI models. ChatGPT and its counterparts are expected to become more finely tuned for specific tasks and industries. Whether it's medical diagnosis, legal document analysis, or engineering support, AI models will increasingly exhibit domain expertise, making them even more valuable in niche applications.

2. Improved Understanding of Context

As AI models continue to evolve, they are likely to exhibit a deeper understanding of context and user intent. This improvement in context-awareness will lead to more accurate and relevant responses, making AI assistance feel even more natural and human-like. It will be a game-changer in fields such as customer support and content creation.

3. Enhanced Collaboration between Humans and AI

The future of AI assistance envisions a collaborative partnership between humans and machines. AI will be a trusted ally, working alongside us to tackle complex challenges. It will serve as a force multiplier, extending our abilities and automating routine tasks, thereby freeing us to focus on creative, strategic, and high-value tasks.

4. Ethical and Responsible AI

The importance of ethical and responsible AI use will continue to be a focal point in the future. As AI's role in our lives expands, so does the need to ensure that it operates in an ethical and unbiased manner. Guidelines and regulations will be further refined to guarantee the responsible use of AI across industries.

5. Integration into Various Industries

AI assistance will become a standard feature in various industries. Businesses will rely on AI models for customer support, data analysis, and decision-making. Educational institutions will leverage AI for personalized learning experiences, and healthcare will benefit from AI-powered diagnostic and treatment support.

6. Evolving Workflows and Productivity

The way we work and interact with technology is poised to change. AI assistance will seamlessly integrate into our workflows, reducing manual and repetitive tasks. The result will be increased productivity and efficiency across diverse professions.

7. Enhanced User Experiences

As AI models become more user-centric, the user experience will take center stage. User interfaces will become even more intuitive, and the quality of AI-generated content will improve, making interactions with AI models more enjoyable and valuable.

8. Customization and Personalization

AI assistance will become increasingly tailored to individual needs. Users will be able to customize their AI models to a greater extent, ensuring that AI understands their unique preferences and requirements.

9. Research and Innovation

The future of AI assistance holds the promise of continued innovation and breakthroughs. Researchers and developers will push the boundaries of what AI can achieve, leading to new and exciting applications that we can't yet foresee.

10. Global Impact

AI assistance is not limited to a specific region; its impact will be global. It will be instrumental in addressing global challenges, enhancing education, healthcare, and cross-cultural communication.

As we look ahead to the future of AI assistance, it is evident that the possibilities are boundless. With the right approach, ethical considerations, and a spirit of innovation, AI will become an invaluable tool that empowers individuals, businesses, and society as a whole. By staying informed, adaptable, and responsible, we can embrace the future of AI assistance with confidence, knowing that it will be a driving force for positive change and progress.

Thank you!

I would like to express my deepest gratitude to all the readers who have chosen "ChatGPT Money Machine: Making AI Work for You" as a valuable resource in their journey to harness the power of AI. Your support and trust in this book mean the world to me.

Writing this book has been a labor of love, and it wouldn't have been possible without the encouragement and enthusiasm of readers like you. Your commitment to exploring the potential of AI and its practical applications is a testament to your dedication to personal and professional growth.

I'd also like to extend my appreciation to the dedicated teams at OpenAI and other organizations that have been at the forefront of AI development. Your tireless efforts in pushing the boundaries of AI technology have paved the way for groundbreaking innovations and continue to inspire us all.

As we navigate the ever-evolving landscape of AI, I hope that the knowledge and insights shared in this book serve as a valuable guide in your pursuit of AI-driven success.

Thank you for your trust and for being a part of this exciting journey into the future of AI assistance. Your feedback, questions, and suggestions are always welcome as we continue to learn and grow together.

Warm regards,